into Science™

Grade 3

All images ©Houghton Mifflin Harcourt, Inc., unless otherwise noted

Cover: ©Arif Suprlyadl/Shutterstock

Printed in the U.S.A.

ISBN 978-0-358-29690-4

6 7 8 9 10 0607 29 28 27 26 25 24 23

4500866092

r2.21

Whose book is this?

_____

Observe the cover.

I notice _____

_____

I wonder _____

_____

A scientist ...

is

can

uses

What does your robot look like?

Science makes me feel ...

I like science because ... _____

_____

_____

_____

Consulting Authors

Michael A. DiSpezio
Global Educator
North Falmouth, Massachusetts

Marjorie Frank
*Science Writer and Content-Area
   Reading Specialist*
Brooklyn, New York

Michael R. Heithaus, PhD
*Dean, College of Arts, Sciences &
   Education Professor, Department
   of Biological Sciences*
Florida International University
Miami, Florida

Peter McLaren
Executive Director of Next Gen Education, LLC
Providence, Rhode Island

Bernadine Okoro
*Social Emotional Learning Consultant
STEM Learning Advocate & Consultant*
Washington, DC

Cary Sneider, PhD
Associate Research Professor
Portland State University
Portland, Oregon

Program Advisors

Paul D. Asimow, PhD
*Eleanor and John R. McMillan Professor of Geology and
   Geochemistry*
California Institute of Technology
Pasadena, California

Eileen Cashman, PhD
Professor of Environmental Resources Engineering
Humboldt State University
Arcata, California

Mark B. Moldwin, PhD
Professor of Climate and Space Sciences and Engineering
University of Michigan
Ann Arbor, Michigan

Kelly Y. Neiles, PhD
Associate Professor of Chemistry
St. Mary's College of Maryland
St. Mary's City, Maryland

Sten Odenwald, PhD
Astronomer
NASA Goddard Spaceflight
   Center
Greenbelt, Maryland

Bruce W. Schafer
Director of K-12 STEM Collaborations, Retired
Oregon University System
Portland, Oregon

Barry A. Van Deman
President and CEO
Museum of Life and Science
Durham, North Carolina

Kim Withers, PhD
Assistant Professor
Texas A&M
   University-Corpus Christi
Corpus Christi, Texas

Classroom Reviewers

Julie Ahern
Andrew Cooke Magnet School
Waukegan, Illinois

Amy Berke
South Park Elementary School
Rapid City, South Dakota

Pamela Bluestein
Sycamore Canyon School
Newbury Park, California

Kelly Brotz
Cooper Elementary School
Sheboygan, Wisconsin

Andrea Brown
HLPUSD Science and STEAM TOSA,
    Retired
Hacienda Heights, California

Marsha Campbell
Murray Elementary School
Hobbs, New Mexico

Leslie C. Antosy-Flores
Star View Elementary School
Midway City, California

Theresa Gailliout
James R. Ludlow Elementary School
Philadelphia, Pennsylvania

Emily Giles
Assistant Principal
White's Tower Elementary School
Independence, KY

Robert Gray
Essex Elementary School
Baltimore, Maryland

Stephanie Greene
Science Department Chair
Sun Valley Magnet School
Sun Valley, California

Roya Hosseini
Junction Avenue K–8 School
Livermore, California

Rana Mujtaba Khan
Will Rogers High School
Van Nuys, California

George Kwong
Schafer Park Elementary School
Hayward, California

Kristin Kyde
Templeton Middle School
Sussex, Wisconsin

Marie LaCross
Sulphur Springs United
    School District
Santa Clarita, California

Bonnie Lock
La Center Elementary School
La Center, Washington

Imelda Madrid
Assistant Principal
Montague Charter Academy for the
    Arts and Sciences
Pacoima, CA

Susana Martinez O'Brien
Diocese of San Diego
San Diego, California

Kara Miller
Ridgeview Elementary School
Beckley, West Virginia

Mercy D. Momary
Local District Northwest
Los Angeles, California

Dena Morosin
Shasta Elementary School
Klamath Falls, Oregon

Craig Moss
Mt. Gleason Middle School
Sunland, California

Joanna O'Brien
Palmyra Elementary School
Palmyra, Missouri

Wendy Savaske
Education Consultant
Wisconsin Department of
    Public Instruction

Isabel Souto
Schafer Park Elementary School
Hayward, California

Michelle Sullivan
Balboa Elementary School
San Diego, California

April Thompson
Roll Hill School
Cincinnati, Ohio

Tina Topoleski
District Science Supervisor
Jackson School District
Jackson, New Jersey

Terri Trebilcock
Fairmount Elementary School
Golden, Colorado

Emily R.C.G. Williams
South Pasadena Middle School
South Pasadena, California

These are some smart people!

Unit 1 Engineering and Technology

Unit 2 Forces and Motion

Unit 3 Life Cycles and Inherited Traits

Unit 4 Organisms and Their Environments 139

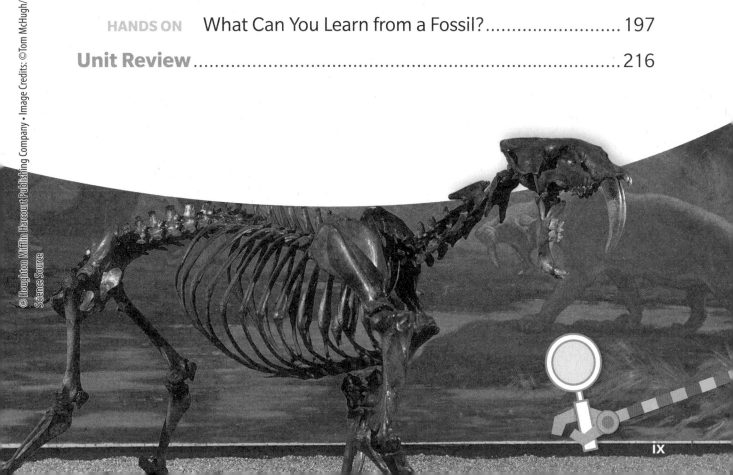

Engineering

Engineers develop solutions for problems. They use an engineering design process to help them find a good solution to a problem. This engineering design process has three main parts, or phases.

PROBLEM → EXPLORE → MAKE and TEST → IMPROVE and TEST → SOLUTION

Explore

Find out more about a problem by asking questions and doing research. Then state the problem clearly. Identify criteria and constraints. A **criterion** is a desirable feature of a solution. A **constraint** is a limit on an acceptable solution. The problem is defined when you state the problem and identify criteria and constraints.

Make and Test

Develop a good solution. This phase can include the following steps:

- Brainstorm
- Plan
- Make
- Test
- Evaluate

Think of as many ideas as you can. These ideas may or may not solve the problem you defined. Choose which solution you think will work best. Then plan and make a prototype to test. A prototype is a model of a solution that can be tested.

Testing a prototype helps you know how well a solution works. If a solution does not solve the problem, change the solution or choose another solution. Test a solution after each change so you know if the change worked as expected. More than one solution may solve a problem. Compare solutions to choose which is best. The solution that best meets the criteria and constraints is the better solution.

Improve and Test

Change a good solution to make it better. You may replan, redesign, and retest many small changes. You may even return to an earlier phase if needed. Always communicate with others to share information or learn more. At the end of the process you should have as good a solution as possible, given the constraints.

Hana wants to attract pretty birds to her backyard. Talk with a partner about how Hana might use an engineering design process to solve this problem.

Claims, Evidence, and Reasoning
Constructing Explanations

A complete scientific explanation needs three parts—a claim, evidence, and reasoning.

A **claim** is a statement you think is true. It answers the question, "What do you know?" **Evidence** is data. It answers the question, "How do you know that?" **Reasoning** tells the connection between the evidence and the claim. It answers the question, "Why does your evidence support your claim?"

You're investigating what mix of baking soda and vinegar makes the largest eruption. You keep the baking soda amount the same and increase the amount of vinegar each time.

You have 50 mL, 100 mL, and 200 mL of vinegar and one tablespoon of baking soda for each container. Before you begin, you make a **claim**.

The largest amount of vinegar will react the most.

You add the baking soda and observe. The data you gather is evidence. It can show if your claim is true or not. Now you're ready to construct a scientific explanation with a claim, **evidence**, and reasoning.

Claim	The largest amount of vinegar will react the most.
Evidence	The container with 200 mL of vinegar made more bubbles than the others.
Reasoning	The evidence showed that more vinegar makes a larger reaction than a little vinegar.

Evidence used to support a claim can be used to make another claim.

You decide to try a different type of investigation. Describe it below. Include a claim, evidence, and reasoning.

My investigation is

Warm vinegar will produce a larger reaction than cold vinegar.

Claim	
Evidence	
Reasoning	

Safety in the Lab

Doing science is a lot of fun. But, a science lab can be a dangerous place. Falls, cuts, and burns can happen easily. **Know the safety rules and listen to your teacher.**

☐ **Think ahead.** Study the investigation steps so you know what to expect. If you have any questions, ask your teacher. Be sure you understand all caution statements and safety reminders.

☐ **Be neat and clean.** Keep your work area clean. If you have long hair, pull it back so it doesn't get in the way. Roll or push up long sleeves to keep them away from your activity.

☐ **Oops!** If you spill or break something, or get cut, tell your teacher right away.

☐ **Watch your eyes.** Wear safety goggles anytime you are directed to do so. If you get anything in your eyes, tell your teacher right away.

☐ **Yuck!** Never eat or drink anything during a science activity.

☐ **Don't get shocked.** Be careful if an electric appliance is used. Be sure that electric cords are in a safe place where you can't trip over them. Never use the cord to pull a plug from an outlet.

☐ **Keep it clean.** Always clean up when you have finished. Put everything away and wipe your work area. Wash your hands.

☐ **Play it safe.** Always know where to find safety equipment, such as fire extinguishers. Know how to use the safety equipment around you.

Safety in the Field

Lots of science research happens outdoors. It's fun to explore the wild! But, you need to be careful. The weather, the land, and the living things can surprise you.

☐ **Think ahead.** Study the investigation steps so you know what to expect. If you have any questions, ask your teacher. Be sure you understand all caution statements and safety reminders.

☐ **Dress right.** Wear appropriate clothes and shoes for the outdoors. Cover up and wear sunscreen and sunglasses for sun safety.

☐ **Clean up the area.** Follow your teacher's instructions for when and how to throw away waste.

☐ **Oops!** Tell your teacher right away if you break something or get hurt.

☐ **Watch your eyes.** Wear safety goggles when directed to do so. If you get anything in your eyes, tell your teacher right away.

☐ **Yuck!** Never taste anything outdoors.

☐ **Stay with your group.** Work in the area as directed by your teacher. Stay on marked trails.

☐ **"Wilderness" doesn't mean go wild.** Never engage in horseplay, games, or pranks.

☐ **Always walk.** No running!

☐ **Play it safe.** Know where safety equipment can be found and how to use it. Know how to get help.

☐ **Clean up.** Wash your hands with soap and water when you come back indoors.

© Houghton Mifflin Harcourt Publishing Company • Image Credits: ©HMH

Safety Symbols

To highlight important safety concerns, the following symbols are used in a Hands-On Activity. Remember that no matter what safety symbols you see, all safety rules should be followed at all times.

Dress Code

- Wear safety goggles as directed.
- If anything gets into your eye, tell your teacher immediately.
- Do not wear contact lenses in the lab.
- Wear appropriate protective gloves as directed.
- Tie back long hair, secure loose clothing, and remove loose jewelry.

Glassware and Sharp Object Safety

- Do not use chipped or cracked glassware.
- Notify your teacher immediately if a piece of glass breaks.
- Use extreme care when handling all sharp and pointed instruments.
- Do not cut an object while holding the object in your hands.
- Cut objects on a suitable surface, always in a direction away from your body.

Electrical Safety

- Do not use equipment with frayed electrical cords or loose plugs.
- Do not use electrical equipment near water or when clothing or hands are wet.
- Hold the plug when you plug in or unplug equipment.

Chemical Safety

- If a chemical gets on your skin, on your clothing, or in your eyes, rinse it immediately, and tell your teacher.
- Do not clean up spilled chemicals unless your teacher directs you to do so.
- Keep your hands away from your face while you are working on any activity.

Heating and Fire Safety

- Know your school's evacuation-fire routes.
- Never leave a hot plate unattended while it is turned on or while it is cooling.
- Allow equipment to cool before storing it.

Plant and Animal Safety

- Do not eat any part of a plant.
- Do not pick any wild plant unless your teacher instructs you to do so.
- Treat animals carefully and respectfully.
- Wash your hands thoroughly after handling any plant or animal.

Cleanup

- Clean all work surfaces and protective equipment as directed by your teacher.
- Wash your hands throughly before you leave the lab or after any activity.

Safety Quiz

Name _____

Circle the letter of the BEST answer.

1. Before starting an activity, you should

    a. try an experiment of your own.

    b. open all containers and packages.

    c. read all directions and make sure you understand them.

    d. handle all the equipment to become familiar with it.

2. At the end of any activity, you should

    a. wash your hands thoroughly before leaving the lab.

    b. cover your face with your hands.

    c. put on your safety goggles.

    d. leave the materials where they are.

3. If you get hurt or injured in any way, you should

    a. tell your teacher immediately.

    b. find bandages or a first aid kit.

    c. go to your principal's office.

    d. get help after you finish the activity.

4. When working with materials that might fly into the air and hurt someone's eye, you should wear

    a. goggles.   **b.** an apron.

    c. gloves.   **d.** a hat.

5. If you get something in your eye, you should

    a. wash your hands immediately.

    b. put the lid back on the container.

    c. wait to see if your eye becomes irritated.

    d. tell your teacher right away.

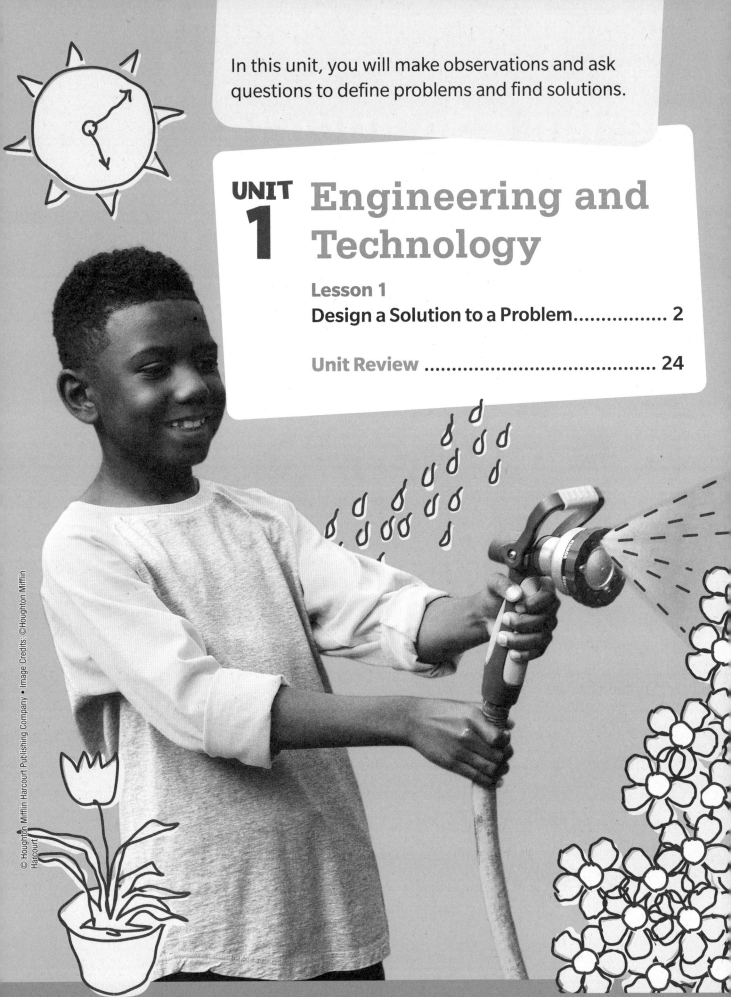

In this unit, you will make observations and ask questions to define problems and find solutions.

UNIT 1 Engineering and Technology

What do you notice about these plants?

I notice _____

_____

_____

What do you wonder about these plants?

I wonder _____

_____

_____

Can You Explain It?

How do you think these plants can be watered when nobody is there? Sketch, write, or model your answer.

Engineer It
Plant Problems

Your class takes care of several plants. A two-week break is coming, and school will be closed. No one will be able to water the plants. Your class wants to design a safe way to water the plants with some basic materials.

Form a question Ask a question about how your class can make sure the plants at school are watered during the two-week break.

© Houghton Mifflin Harcourt Publishing Company • Image Credits: (c) ©George Clerk/iStockPhoto.com

POSSIBLE MATERIALS

- ☐ safety goggles
- ☐ gloves, apron
- ☐ soda bottles
- ☐ plastic cups
- ☐ milk jugs, empty, clean
- ☐ water-absorbent materials
- ☐ rubber bands
- ☐ containers for water
- ☐ water
- ☐ tape

Explore

STEP 1   **Identify**   What is the problem you need to solve?

_____

_____

Criteria are the desirable features of a solution. What are two possible criteria for your solution?

_____

_____

_____

Constraints are the limits on a solution. What is one possible constraint on your solution?

_____

_____

STEP 2   **Research**   Find different examples of ways plants can be watered when people aren't around. List two examples below.

_____

_____

_____

Make and Test

STEP 3 **Make** Think of your own solution to the problem. Draw your idea below.

  Discuss with your group ways that you can give feedback without making someone feel bad.

STEP 4 **Share** Discuss your solution with your group. Explain how each solution meets the criteria and constraints of the problem.

STEP 5 **Design a solution** Combine features of each idea to develop your team's solution. With your team, draw the solution on a separate sheet of paper.

STEP 6 **Develop a model** Use your drawing to build a prototype of your solution. A prototype is a model used for testing.

STEP 7 **Make a plan** Write a plan to test how much water your solution gives to the plant.

STEP 8 **Collect data** Carry out your test three times.

STEP 9 **Organize data** Complete the data table below.

Trial	Amount of water released (mL)	Observations
1		
2		
3		

How well does the prototype meet the criteria and constraints?

Draw conclusions Make a **claim** about one advantage and one limitation of your proposed solution. Support your claim with **evidence** from your investigation and explain your **reasoning.**

Making Sense

How did planning, developing, and testing a solution to water plants help you begin to understand how engineers solve problems?

Engineer It
Looking It Over

No solution is perfect. Failure helps us identify ways we can improve a solution. Sometimes, one part of a solution is changed. Other times, a new solution may be developed. This process is known as redesigning.

Form a question Ask a question about how your team can improve its watering system solution.

Did you know?

The space shuttle was frequently modified for 30 years!

Improve and Test

STEP 1   **Identify** Go back to your drawing of the team solution. Circle areas where it failed or could be improved.

STEP 2   **Improve** Think of ways that you can improve your solution. What changes will you make to your prototype?

How do these changes better meet the criteria and constraints?

_____

_____

_____

STEP 3   **Make a model** Draw and label your improved solution. Point out the ways your improved solution differs from your original solution.

STEP 4   **Redesign** Modify your prototype based on the changes in your new model.

STEP 5 **Collect data** Test your improved prototype. Record your observations below.

STEP 6 **Analyze data** Describe how well your improved prototype solves the problem. How well did it meet the criteria and constraint for a good solution?

Draw conclusions Make a **claim** about the importance of redesign. Support your claim with **evidence** from your investigation and explain your **reasoning.**

Making Sense

How did following the steps of this investigation help you explain how engineers develop new technologies and improve existing ones?

Exploring Engineering Problems

Where Do Solutions Come from?

When faced with problems, engineers can help. **Engineers** design solutions to meet a want or need.

You use technology many times a day! But do you know what technology is? **Technology** is human-made devices or systems that meet a want or need. People's wants and needs change over time, so there is always a need for new and improved technology.

This is a tablet. It can store many books or magazines in one device. It can also address other wants and needs.

What want or need did the tablet solve?

Not all technology is electric. This tent keeps you dry when you sleep outside.

Zippers are a form of technology, too. They hold fabric together.

This ball is technology, too! It can be rolled, kicked, or thrown.

With a partner, find two human-made items in your classroom. Identify the needs they meet.

_____

_____

_____

Engineers design, develop, and improve technology using the engineering design process. This process includes exploring a problem, making and testing solutions, and improving a solution.

PROBLEM → EXPLORE → MAKE and TEST → IMPROVE and TEST → SOLUTION

How Do You Explore a Problem?

The first step in the design process is to identify a problem. Before you can work on solving a problem, you should clearly know what you need or want. This will make solving the problem easier.

When you design a solution, you need to know what the solution must include or be able to do. These desirable features of the solution are the criteria.

Recycling is good for the planet. Your school bought recycle bins to put in each class to reduce the amount of garbage going to the landfill. On Fridays, students collect the bins. Sometimes, the bins are so heavy they are hard to lift easily and safely. You and your classmates have been asked to find a way to easily and safely move the bins on Fridays.

What is the problem about the bins that needs to be solved?

_____

_____

What are two criteria for designing better bins?

_____

_____

Finding the Limits

Part of solving an engineering problem is identifying the constraints. Constraints are limits on acceptable solutions, which may include limits on available resources. People don't have endless amounts of time, money, or materials to solve a problem.

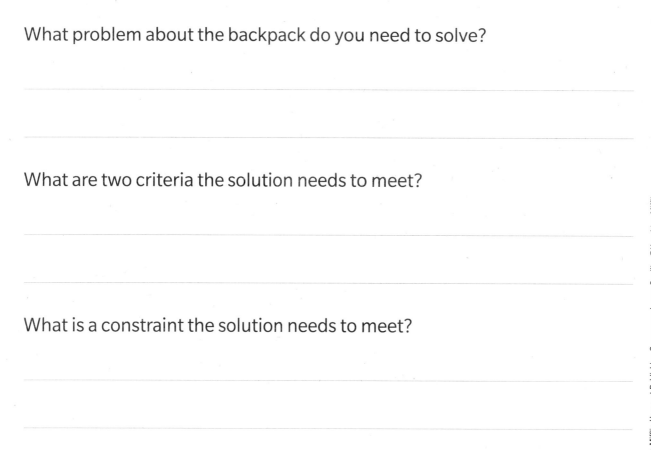

There are times you need to bring more supplies to school than usual. Not all backpacks are big enough to hold all your supplies and they can be hard to carry. It is important that the backpack closes. You don't want your supplies to fall out!

What problem about the backpack do you need to solve?

_____

_____

What are two criteria the solution needs to meet?

_____

_____

What is a constraint the solution needs to meet?

_____

_____

 Discuss with a partner a problem you have faced and how you solved it. Ask them how they might solve it. Sometimes, the best way to solve a new problem is to look at how others have solved similar problems.

Researching Solutions

People have worked to find different ways to water plants for a long time. Different situations require different solutions. Some solutions to the problem are shown below.

Sprinkler systems water farms. This provides a lot of water over a very large area.

Drip hoses let out tiny drips of water near the hose. This allows a lot of plants to be watered along the hose.

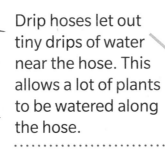

Watering spikes slowly pass water into soil. This keeps the plant from getting too much water.

Making Sense

How do the steps you learned about help you understand the way engineers might work to solve different problems?

Making and Testing Solutions

After you have defined the problem and done research, it's time to brainstorm a solution. When coming up with a solution, don't limit yourself to just one answer. Think of several solutions and then decide on the one that you think best solves the problem!

Peer Review

Teamwork is an important part of most engineering and science work. Getting and giving advice can often lead to better solutions. In order to select the best solution, engineers consider how each solution meets the criteria and constraints. This information is used to create a team solution. This solution often includes components of each individual design.

Make a Prototype

After choosing a solution, it's time to make a working model, or prototype. Models can be built in many ways. Some can be produced by 3D printers. Others are made by hand using materials that are available.

Engineering Tests

Designing a solution for watering plants requires attention to detail, constraints, criteria, and many other important things. Professional engineers make sure to do the same with their solutions. Look at each picture to learn more about some of the ways professional engineers plan and test their solutions.

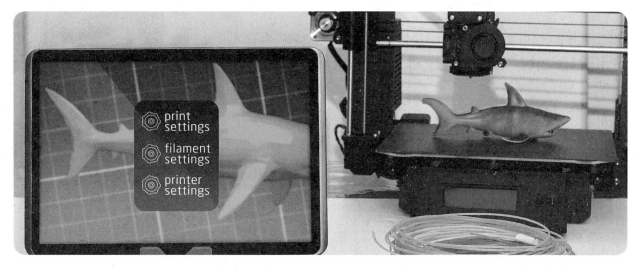

Some engineers use 3D printers to make prototypes to see what their ideas might look like and how the final product might function.

3D printing enables a fast, inexpensive prototype. So, a prosthetic hand design can be made, tested, and remade until it's an exact fit.

Small-scale models are tested to see if a solution will work. Often, these models don't include all the details of the actual solution.

Where Things Break

Testing often reveals flaws in the original solution. Engineers learn from these failures. Failures are a way to make better and safer solutions. The bridge in this image is over the very windy Tacoma Narrows in Washington. It collapsed on November 7, 1940.

Identify List two potential problems that could have caused the bridge to collapse.

Learning from Failure

Problems happen often. Even the best engineers can't predict every problem or failure that will happen. The thing to do is to plan ahead to avoid as many problems as possible.

Part of being an engineer is learning to accept that things get better after a failure. Finding out what went wrong—and why—can help improve the solution. Sometimes, you only need to make small changes. In other cases, you need to redesign and test many times before a solution works well.

Making Sense

How does analyzing failure help you understand how engineers can continuously improve solutions?

Improving Over Time

Getting Advice

As engineers, it is important to have other engineers and experts look at our work, too. Think about a bridge and what makes the best solution for its purpose.

Collaborate As a group, design a paper bridge that spans a 12-inch space and can hold one pound. Then, build and test your solution. Share your solution and the results of your testing with the class.

Evaluate your solution and the solutions of four other groups by entering the information in the table. Make sure to rate the solutions with a five-star rating. One star is the lowest rating, and five stars is the highest rating. Give reasons for your ratings in the table.

Team	Rating	Reason for rating

Reflect What did you learn from reviewing your classmates' solutions?

Improving Together

Evaluating solutions isn't as easy as riding a bike or following a recipe. There are many things to think about. Often the best solution may come from looking at many different solutions and taking the best ideas from each one. Sometimes, this is the best way to meet the criteria and constraints.

It is always important to communicate and record information about your solution. Also, keep track of any lessons you learned along the way. Even if you feel that you have finished, you may still have work to do.

Evaluate Think of your bridge solution. Now, think of your classmates' solutions that you evaluated. Describe an improved solution that combines the best features from all the different solutions.

_____

_____

_____

Making Sense

How does learning about working together help you understand how engineers improve solutions?

_____

_____

_____

Lesson Check

Can You Explain It?

Remember that the school will be closed for a long break. No one can care for the plants during the break. Explain how you would solve the problem. Be sure to include the following:

- Explain the importance of researching past solutions.
- Describe how you developed your proposed solution, and explain why you communicated with others about your solution.
- Understand what to consider when testing a possible solution.

Now I know or think that _____

_____

_____

Making Connections

You are going out of town and cannot take your pet. You need to make a way for your pet to get food and water. How is this problem like the problem at the beginning of the lesson? How is it different?

_____

_____

Checkpoints

Use the images below to answer the questions.

1. The boats above were designed for different purposes. List one criteria and one constraint for each boat. You may use the same answer more than once.

Type of boat	Criteria	Constraint
speedboat		
sailboat		
canoe		

2. Tracy needs a boat to fish in a pond. The boat should be small, quiet, and easy to move. Compare the boats above and explain which best meets Tracy's needs.

3. Identify one possible failure that could occur with all of the boats? How could engineers make an improvement to reduce this risk?

Use the images below to answer the questions.

Bridge A

Bridge B

4. Make a claim about which of the bridges above is best designed for the boats on the previous page. Cite evidence from the images and explain your reasoning.

_____

_____

_____

5. You design a solution to a problem. What must you do before you can test it?

a. research

b. brainstorm

c. make a model

d. define the problem

Unit Review

1. Look at the image. What is the unmet want or need shown in the scene?

   a. having air in the tire to ride on safely

   b. reducing the number of bikes on the road

   c. walking instead of riding a bike

   d. not having someone around to help change a flat tire

2. A school needs new desks for their students. Identify two criteria and one constraint that the school must consider when buying a new desk.

   _____

   _____

   _____

3. A grocery store needs a new shopping cart. They have three solutions to choose from. What type of data would help you choose the best cart? Circle all correct answers.

   a. How many carts the store needs

   b. How easy it is to push

   c. How much food the shopping cart can hold

   d. How long it takes to make the shopping cart

4. Based on this image, what is the best solution to the problem?

    a. digging up the plant and throwing it away

    b. finding a way to get water to the plant

    c. keeping the plant away from animals that may eat it

    d. designing a way to hold the plant up straight

5. Identify a problem that computers solve. How do different computers meet different needs?

_____

_____

_____

6. This school wants to install a safer swing set. Explain how communication and teamwork will help an engineer design the best solution.

_____

_____

_____

7. Look at the image. What problem or need were shoes developed to solve?

_____

_____

_____

8. Circle the image below that shows the best solution for fixing this broken shoe. Then make a claim about why it is the best solution.

_____

_____

9. Tell what evidence from the images supports your claim and explain your reasoning.

_____

_____

10. Explain why the other two solutions would not be the best for fixing the shoe.

_____

_____

_____

In Unit 1, you observed how forces can cause problems or may provide solutions. In this unit, you will plan and carry out investigations on forces to discover how forces can cause or change motion.

UNIT 2 Forces and Motion

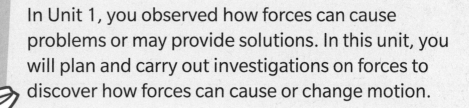

Snow way!
Look at him go!

What do you notice about this sled?

I notice _____

_____

_____

_____

What do you wonder about what makes this sled move?

I wonder _____

_____

_____

_____

Can You Explain It?

How do forces affect this sled's motion? Sketch, write, or model your answer.

Move the Car

A lot of people like to watch car races. Forces make these race cars move very fast! A **force** is a push or pull on a specific object. The strength of a force affects an object's motion. You will explore the effects of forces.

Form a question Ask a question about how the strength of a force affects the way a vehicle moves.

> **Did you know?**
>
> The forces on some race cars can make them move at speeds of over 320 km/hr (200 mph)!

POSSIBLE MATERIALS

☐ toy vehicle

☐ tape measure

☐ masking tape

☐ stopwatch

STEP 1 **Investigate your question** Look at the materials. How do you think they help you collect data to answer your question?

Determine how you will measure the effects of weak, medium, and strong forces on a vehicle. Make sure you only change one factor, or variable, in your investigation. Write your group's plan below. Get your teacher's approval.

STEP 2 **Organize your data** Carry out your plan. Record your data on the next page.

Carry out your plan a second time. Why is it important to control the variables you test and test multiple times?

Use the space below to record your data.

STEP 3 **Analyze your data**
What is your evidence
that you did not apply the
same strength of force for
each push?

Explain how a change in forces causes the vehicle to move
differently.

Make a **claim** about what caused the differences in the way the vehicle moved from one trial to the next. Support your claim with **evidence** from your investigation and explain your **reasoning**.

_____

_____

_____

Making Sense

Share your claim with others. Revise your claim based on their feedback, if needed. How does your evidence help explain the way forces affect the movement of the sled?

_____

_____

_____

 Tell how your group was able to share the tasks for this activity in a way that included everyone.

_____

_____

Ramp Moves

Objects that touch exert forces on each other. **Friction** is a force that can slow objects down as they rub together. Think about how friction affects the people on this slide.

Form a question Ask a question about how materials affect the amount of friction between two objects.

Did you know?

Friction produces heat. As objects rub together, they get warmer.

POSSIBLE MATERIALS

- [ ] cardboard
- [ ] aluminum foil
- [ ] tape
- [ ] various materials for testing
- [ ] coin
- [ ] meterstick
- [ ] rulers

Investigate your question Cover a piece of cardboard with aluminum foil and tape it. Tape the cardboard to your desk. Then, set a coin at the edge. Slowly raise the edge. Measure the height at which the coin begins to move. Place the coin on various materials, such as felt or rubber. Then, try again. Record your results in the table.

Draw conclusions Make a **claim** about friction between different materials. Explain how the **evidence** and your reasoning support your **claim**.

Type of material	Height of ramp

Making Sense

How does this activity help you explain the effect of friction on the sled as it moves down the hill?

Which Way?

The direction in which a force is applied matters as much as how strong the force is. When you push something, you use force to move it away from you. When you pull something, you use force to move it toward you. However, more than one force can act on an object at the same time. These forces may be applied in the same or different directions.

The dogs are playing a game like tug of war. They are each applying a force in the opposite direction.

Carefully Balanced

Pairs of forces are either balanced or unbalanced. **Balanced forces** are the same strength but act in opposite directions, so there is no change in motion. When one force is stronger than the other and the forces act in different directions, they are **unbalanced forces**.

Explain Circle the image below that shows a change in motion. Use an arrow to show the direction of motion.

The two dogs are evenly matched. They both pull with a force of 10. The X marks the center of the rope at the start. The rope hasn't moved, even though both dogs are pulling.

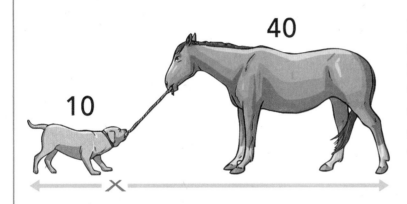

Now, one dog is playing tug of war with a big horse. The horse is stronger and pulls with a force of 40. The dog will be pulled over the X in the direction of the horse.

You can add all the forces that push or pull on an object. This sum is called **net force**. If the animals pull with equal force, the forces are balanced. This is zero net force. The motion does not change.

Predict who will win in a battle of tug of war and say whether the forces are balanced or unbalanced.

Force A	Force B	Winner	Balanced or unbalanced?
big horse	big horse		
big horse	adult elephant		
big horse	goat		

Direction Matters

You know that the direction that a force is applied is important. In air hockey, hitting the puck in the wrong direction could make you lose the game!

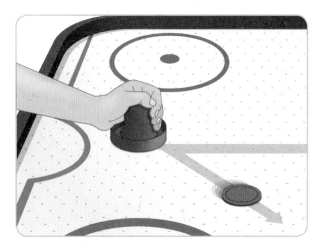

Players use mallets to apply forces to the puck.

The force of the mallet changes the direction of the puck and sends it into the other goal.

A still object has balanced forces acting on it. Balanced forces also are acting on a moving object that does not change speed or direction. When a moving object changes direction or speed, unbalanced forces are acting on it.

Making Sense

How do balanced and unbalanced forces help explain the sled's motion as it starts moving down the hill?

What Are Contact Forces?

Friction on a zipline is low until you are near the end of the ride. Then the braking system adds friction. That friction brings the rider to a comfortable, safe stop.

Remember that friction occurs as objects rub together. One way people use this force is to stop objects. The zipline brakes rub against the cable to stop the rider. Car brakes work in a similar way to stop moving vehicles.

Making Sense

How do contact forces help explain why the sled stops moving at the bottom of the hill?

Gravity Can Bring You Down

Look at the images below. Predict what you think will happen next to the pizza dough and the basketball.

This pizza cook is tossing a pizza dough to prepare it for baking.

This girl is throwing the ball up at the basket. If it goes in, she scores!

If you predicted that the crust and ball would begin falling back down, you were right! Gravity is the force that pulls things down toward the center of Earth.

Gravity is always acting on objects. It's the reason you walk on the floor instead of the ceiling!

 List steps you could take to test your answer to the question above. Then share them with a classmate.

Gravity and Other Forces

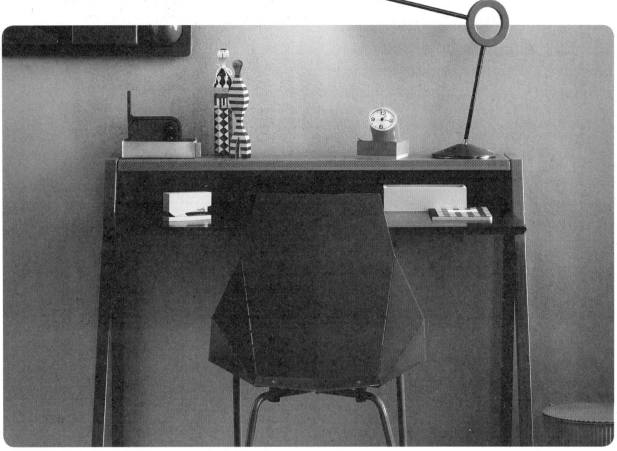

The force of gravity is acting on all of the objects that you can see in this image.

Look at the objects on the desk. Gravity is pulling on them, but they are not falling to the floor. Another force is keeping them from falling to the ground.

Use evidence from the image to explain what force is causing the objects to stay off the ground.

Gravity and Net Force

An object's weight is the strength of gravity's pull on it. A large rock is heavier than a pillow. Gravity pulls down on the rock more forcefully. The rock is hard to lift. To lift the rock, you must apply an upward force on the rock that is greater than gravity's downward force. A rocket is very heavy. It takes a large unbalanced force to overcome the force of gravity and move a rocket away from Earth.

The force of the rocket's engines push up on the rocket. The net force is in an upward direction.

Making Sense

Think about the forces acting on the sled. How does gravity affect the motion of the sled?

_____

_____

Lesson Check

Can You Explain It?

Review your ideas about the sled from the beginning of this lesson. How have your ideas changed? Be sure to do the following:

- Identify the forces that cause the sled to move.
- Explain how gravity and friction affect the motion of the sled.
- Describe how the strength and direction of forces on the sled can change.

Now I know or think that _____

_____

_____

_____

Making Connections

A skateboard uses wheels to move down a ramp. How is this similar to the sled at the beginning of the lesson? How is it different?

_____

_____

_____

Checkpoints

1. Look at each situation. Match the force with its effect in each situation.

Force	Situation	Effect
Friction	Water in a fountain goes up and then comes back down.	Change in speed
Gravity	A person uses the brakes to stop a bicycle.	Change in direction

2. You perform an experiment to see how long it takes a box to slide down three different surfaces. Based on the data below, which surface has the most friction? Cite evidence to explain your reasoning.

| Time to Slide Down a Surface ||
Surface	Time (s)
A	8
B	2
C	5

3. This box is not moving. Predict the motion of the box if two more students push with this student. Explain.

4. Nick and Chris are pushing the same object. Nick pushes it to the right and Chris pushes it to the left. The object moves to the left. Explain what causes this.

_____

_____

5. Which measurement could you make to see how the strength of a force affects a car's motion? Circle all the correct answers.

a. the distance the car travels

b. the color of the car

c. the speed of the car

d. the size of the car's wheels

6. Identify the forces acting on these cards and explain why they are not falling over.

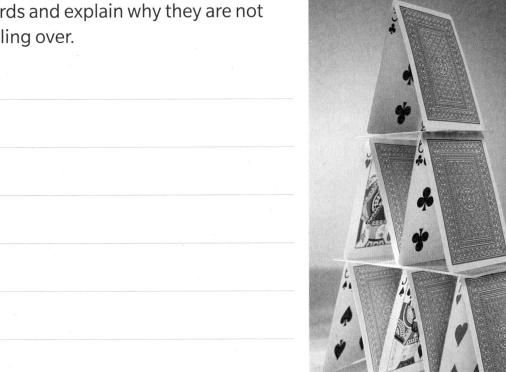

_____

_____

_____

_____

Motion

How does
he do that?

What do you notice about the balls this juggler is using?

I notice _____

_____

_____

What do you wonder about the motion of these balls?

I wonder _____

_____

_____

Can You Explain It?

How do jugglers learn to predict the locations of moving objects? Sketch, write, or model your answer.

Move It

Different objects move in different ways. Some objects move up and down. Others move side to side. Look around you. What other types of motion do you see?

Form a question Ask a question about the different ways an object can move.

Did you know?

Cotton candy machines use circular motions to make a sweet treat.

POSSIBLE MATERIALS

☐ classroom objects

Investigate your question Walk around your classroom. Identify three objects that move in different ways. List them below. Draw a picture that shows how each object moves.

Draw conclusions Make a **claim** about the ways objects can move based on what you observed. Cite **evidence** to support your claim, and explain your **reasoning**.

Making Sense

How did exploring the motion of objects help you understand how jugglers use motion?

Tick Tock

The ship in this photo is a pendulum. Can you think of a pendulum you have seen before? A playground swing is also a pendulum! Different variables, like length and weight, can affect the motion of a pendulum.

Form a question Ask a question about the motion of a pendulum.

Did you know?

A wrecking ball is a huge pendulum used to knock down walls.

POSSIBLE MATERIALS

- ☐ scissors
- ☐ tape measure
- ☐ string
- ☐ stopwatch
- ☐ washers, large
- ☐ washers, small

STEP 1 **Make a plan** Think about your question. Decide which variable you can test to answer your question. Which variable will you test?

 If your group would like to test more than one variable, what is a good strategy for fairly deciding which variable to test first? Turn to your partner and discuss.

Predict the effect you think your variable will have on the motion of each pendulum.

STEP 2 **Investigate your question** Be careful when using scissors. First, cut two pieces of string. Then knot one end of each string to a washer, forming two pendulums. If the height from which the pendulum is released is not what you are testing, be sure to release each pendulum from the same height. Choose one pendulum, and release it!!

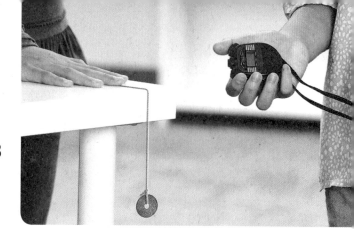

STEP 3 **Organize your data** Use the space below to make a data table and record your results. Repeat Steps 2 and 3 using the second pendulum.

STEP 4 **Analyze your data** Compare your data with the class. Look for patterns in the results.

Draw conclusions Make a **claim** about how the variable you tested affects the pattern of motion of the pendulum. Cite **evidence** from your data, and explain your **reasoning**.

Making Sense

How does understanding repeated motion help you explain how juggling works?

Patterns in Speed and Direction

Patterns, Patterns Everywhere

Patterns of motion happen when the same motion repeats over and over. A merry-go-round spins in a circle. A swimmer uses a backstroke across a pool. A swing goes back and forth.

PICTURES OF MOTION

Learn about the pattern of some motions in these pictures

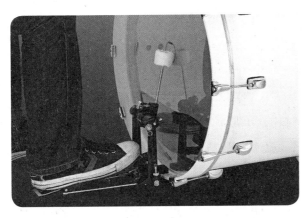

Moving your foot up and down on a drum pedal causes the beater to move forward and hit the drum.

Gravity pulls the pogo stick down and the spring pushes it back up.

A kid zigzags between posts in an obstacle course.

A gust of air causes a pinwheel to spin around.

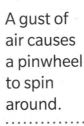

Your Turn

Describe Write or draw an example of each type of motion in the chart.

Back and forth	Spinning	Up and down	Zigzag

How Will It Move?

When you observe a pattern of motion, you can predict how an object will move next. You can predict that the hands of a clock will continue to move in a circle. But you cannot predict a butterfly's next movement. Read about the motions happening in these images.

The toy train's motion is easy to predict, because it will go where the track is. You can see exactly where it will go next.

Divers bounce to go up, and then they fall into the pool. They may twist or flip. That part of their motion is not predictable.

A scuba diver's movements are random. You can't predict if he or she will move up and down, back and forth, in a circle, or in a zigzag motion.

The only thing you can predict about the way an animal chases its prey is that there will be many changes in its speed and direction.

PREDICTIONS

For each situation, make a prediction of what you think will happen next. Write your answer in the table. Then, circle the motions that have a predictable pattern.

Situation	What motion will happen next?
a merry-go-round	
a window washer starting work at the top of a tall building	
an adult rocking a baby in a rocking chair	
a snow skier moving down a hill, making a wavy path	

Analyze In everyday life, you make predictions about motion all the time. You notice whether or not your predictions are correct. Predict the motion for each situation to tell whether or not it is a pattern.

Situation	Pattern	No pattern
A piece of toast being lowered into the toaster.		
The wheels on a bus while the bus is moving.		
A soccer player during a game.		
A basketball being dribbled by a player.		

 Think about how you could help a classmate who is struggling to complete the table above. Turn to a partner and discuss your thoughts.

Making Sense

How do patterns of motion help you explain the way a juggler predicts the location of a ball being juggled?

_____

_____

_____

© Houghton Mifflin Harcourt Publishing Company

Lesson Check

Can You Explain It?

Review your ideas from the beginning of this lesson about how jugglers use motion. How have your ideas changed? Be sure to do the following:

- Explain what type of motion is used while juggling.
- Describe how repeated motion affects the juggler.
- Explain how a pattern makes you able to predict a juggler's motion.

Now I know or think that _____

_____

_____

Making Connections

A Ferris wheel is a popular carnival attraction. It moves around, carrying people from the ground to a point high in the air. How is this like the juggler at the beginning of the lesson? How is it different?

_____

_____

_____

Checkpoints

1. You are on a playground and need to walk by students on swings. How can you predict when it will be safe to go by?

_____

_____

2. Observe the girl jumping on the trampoline. Use your observations as evidence to predict where she will go next.

_____

_____

3. Corrin is jumping rope outside. What pattern of motion tells her when to jump?

_____

_____

_____

4. What type of motions does a yo-yo show? Circle all the correct answers.

   a. zigzag

   b. circular

   c. up and down

   d. back and forth

You investigate how the length of a pendulum affects its motion by making and testing two pendulums. Use the results in the table below to answer questions 5 and 6.

Pendulum	Weight (kg)	Length (cm)	Time (sec)	Number of Swings
Brown	1	40	15	9
Blue	1	60	15	5

5. Predict how you could make a pendulum that swings seven times. Support your reasoning with evidence.

_____

_____

_____

6. Ask a question about the information in the table. Plan an investigation that could answer your question. Be sure to tell which variable you will be testing.

_____

_____

_____

LESSON 3

Forces that Act from a Distance

Whatever floats your...magnet?

What do you notice about these rings?

I notice _____

_____

_____

_____

What do you wonder about the way these rings are interacting?

I wonder _____

_____

_____

_____

Can You Explain It?

How are these rings interacting? Sketch, write, or model your answer.

Solve a Magnet Problem

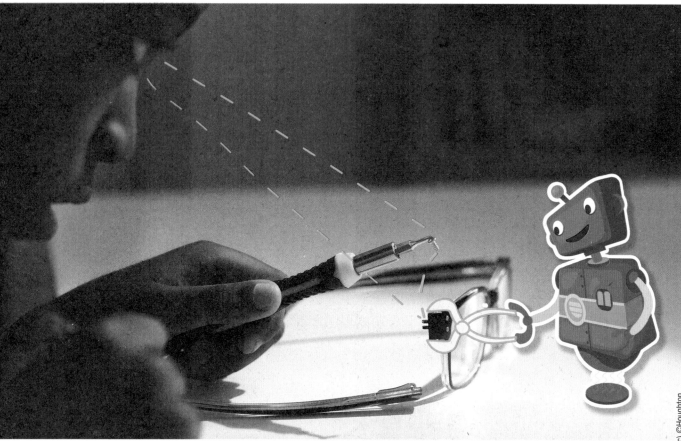

Engineers rely on the properties of magnets to make or improve many tools. A **magnet** is an object that attracts things made from certain metals. Some screwdrivers are now magnetic. This helps hold the metal screw in place while the student works on the glasses.

Form a question Ask a question about the ways magnets interact with other objects.

Did you know?

Metal detectors use magnetic fields to find lost items in the ground!

POSSIBLE MATERIALS

- ☐ bar magnet
- ☐ various classroom objects

STEP 1 **Investigate your question** Look at the objects on your table. Use the magnet to see how it affects the objects.

With your group, develop a way to separate the objects into groups using the magnet.

Describe your plan in the space below.

STEP 2 **Analyze your data** Follow your plan. Then, analyze your results and write a cause-and-effect statement based on your observations.

STEP 3 **Draw conclusions** Think about your observations. What pattern do you notice between the magnet and the objects?

Ask a new question you could investigate based on your results.

Make a **claim** about another problem that could be solved using a magnet. Use **evidence** from your observations to support your claim. Explain your **reasoning**.

Making Sense

How does this activity help you better understand how the ring magnets interact?

Build an Electromagnet

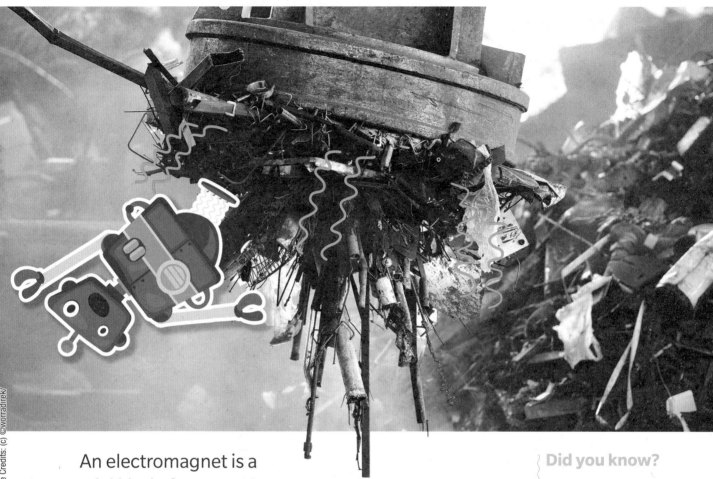

An electromagnet is a special kind of magnet. It can be turned off and on with electricity. The strength of an electromagnet changes depending upon how it's built.

Form a question Ask a question about the strength of an electromagnet.

© Houghton Mifflin Harcourt Publishing Company • Image Credits: (c) ©worradirek7/ Shutterstock

Did you know?

The world's strongest magnet is about the size of a soda can.

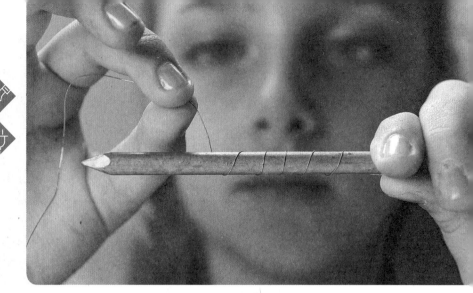

POSSIBLE MATERIALS

- [ ] insulated wire
- [ ] battery holders
- [ ] nail
- [ ] bolt
- [ ] 2 D-cell batteries
- [ ] tape
- [ ] small metal paper clips

STEP 1

Make a plan Gather your materials. Wrap the wire 5 times around a large nail or bolt.

CAUTION: Be careful of the nail's sharp end. Only connect the wire to the battery while testing your electromagnet.

Why do you think you must use a nail or a bolt in the electromagnet?

_____

_____

STEP 2

Investigate your question Connect the wire to the two ends of a battery holder. **CAUTION:** Disconnect the wire from the battery between tests of the magnet. Insert one battery into a battery holder. Place the nail or bolt near the paper clips. Describe what happens.

_____

_____

© Houghton Mifflin Harcourt Publishing Company • Image Credits: (tr) ©Houghton Mifflin Harcourt

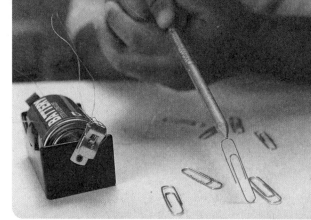

STEP 3 **Organize your data** Record how many paper clips your electromagnet picked up.

STEP 4 **Analyze your data** Compare your results to other groups. What cause-and-effect relationship does the data show?

STEP 5 **Make a plan** Change your electromagnet so that it can pick up more paper clips. Write a new question that you can ask based on the results of your previous test.

Use the space below to record your plan.

Share your plan with your teacher and with permission, try it out. Remember to record your results.

Describe the cause-and-effect relationship between the variable you tested and the number of paper clips the electromagnet picked up.

_____

_____

_____

Why is it important to control the variables and test multiple times?

_____

_____

_____

 Turn to a partner and discuss how you resolved any disagreements in your group.

Draw conclusions Make a **claim** about factors that affect the strength of an electromagnet. Cite **evidence** from your data to support your claim. Explain your **reasoning**.

_____

_____

_____

Making Sense

How does understanding electromagnets help you understand how the ring magnets interact?

_____

_____

Magnets Everywhere!

You know that gravity affects objects from a distance. Other forces also act from a distance. A magnet, for example, can apply a force without touching an object. You may have seen or used magnets at home or at school. Can you find all the magnets in this house?

Speakers have magnets that help create sound waves in the air.

Refrigerators used to close with latches. Now magnets keep most refrigerator doors closed.

A vacuum's motor has magnets in it. The magnets help turn the fan to create suction.

What Pulls to the Poles?

The shape of a magnet may be a horseshoe, a bar, a button, or another form. No matter the shape, every magnet has two poles: north and south. The magnetic force is strongest near a magnet's poles.

FORCE FIELD

Iron filings are small bits of iron. They can be used to show the area around a magnet in which the force pulls or pushes. The magnet has a magnetic field that exerts a force on the filings.

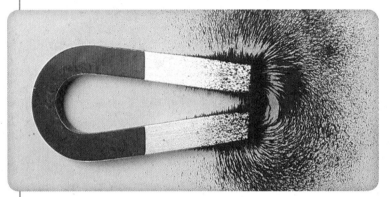

The metal filings show that the strongest part of the magnetic field is at the tips of the horseshoe magnet.

The magnetic field of the bar magnet is strongest at each end and not as strong in the middle.

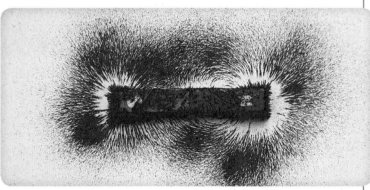

This neodymium magnet has a magnetic field that is equally strong in all directions!

Pushing Away or Pulling Toward

Magnets can pull on, or attract, each other. Or they can push away, or repel, each other. Read the questions to complete a caption for each set of pictures.

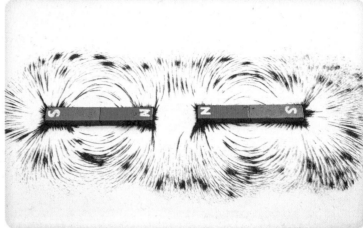

The north poles are alike. Do they repel or attract each other? What do the filings show?

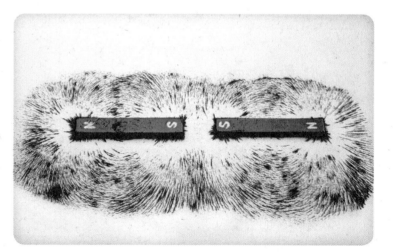

The south poles are alike. Do they repel or attract each other? What do the filings show?

 Turn to a partner and ask how he or she felt when working on these pages. Listen closely to the answer.

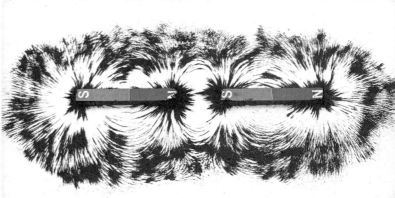

The north and south poles are opposite. Do they repel or attract each other? What do the filings show?

_____

_____

ATTRACT OR REPEL?

How do the magnetic poles of the bar magnets affect the way they interact with each other? Write or draw your observations.

Does Distance Matter?

From what distance do magnets attract the most paper clips?

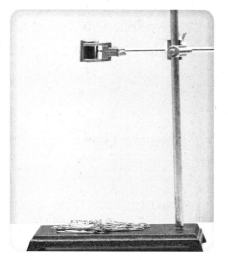

20 cm away

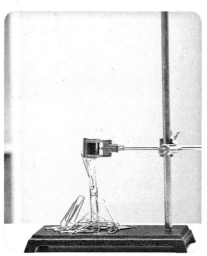

10 cm away

5 cm away

Look at the pattern in the images above. What is causing more paper clips to be attracted to the magnet?

_____

_____

_____

Making Sense

How does knowing about the way magnetic poles interact help you better understand what is happening with the ring magnets?

_____

_____

_____

It's Electric!

Electricity can make things move! **Electricity** is a form of energy. It comes to your home from energy-generating stations. It travels through wires to electrical outlets in your building, ready to be used.

Coal is a fossil fuel that can be burned to produce electrical energy.

At this energy-generating station, heat from burning coal provides the energy to spin a generator.

Electrical energy flows great distances from generating stations through electric lines, such as these.

Electrical energy flows short distances to homes and businesses through electric lines, such as these.

Zap! Static Electricity!

Another type of electricity is static electricity. Static electricity is a charge that builds up on an object. Charges can be positive or negative.

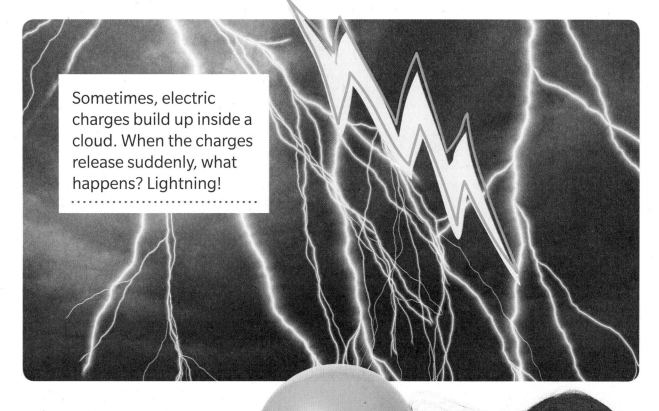

Sometimes, electric charges build up inside a cloud. When the charges release suddenly, what happens? Lightning!

When you rub a balloon against your clothing and then put it near your head, it could be hair-raising!

Recall how magnets can pull or push, attract or repel. Static charges also attract or repel. In magnets, two like poles repel each other. In static electricity, two like charges repel each other, too. Two opposite charges attract each other.

Jump, Spark!

Like magnetic force, electric force can act across a distance. And like a magnet, electricity can produce a field—an electric field. An electric field is strongest nearest the charged object. Van de Graaff machines, such as the ones shown here, make a field of static electricity.

The attraction is strong enough to pull a charge across the gap. You see (and maybe feel) a spark!

Making Sense

How does knowing the way electric forces work help you understand how the rings interact?

Lesson Check

Can You Explain It?

Review your ideas from the beginning of this lesson about how the ring magnets are interacting. How have your ideas changed? Be sure to do the following:

- Identify the force involved in the interaction of these magnets.
- Identify factors that can affect the strength of this force.

Now I know or think that _____

_____

_____

Making Connections

If you touch a Van de Graaff machine, your hair stands up. How is this like the magnets at the beginning of the lesson? How is it different?

_____

_____

1. You have a bowl that contains a rubber ball, a metal key, a safety pin, and a crayon. If you place a magnet above the bowl, what effect will it have on the items in the bowl? Cite evidence to support your reasoning.

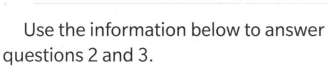

Use the information below to answer questions 2 and 3.

You create an electromagnet that has a wire coiled around a nail three times. You place the magnet a certain distance from a set of paper clips and then turn on your electromagnet. The number of paper clips attracted to the magnet from different distances are shown below.

Distance from paper clips (cm)	Number of paper clips attracted to magnet
1	8
5	6
9	4
12	2

2. Write a cause-and-effect statement based on the patterns in the data.

3. Write a new question that you could investigate based on the patterns in the data.

4. Look at the photo. What do you observe about the stream of water? Explain why this is happening.

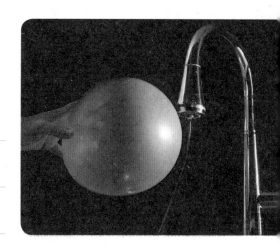

_____

_____

_____

5. What effects show that forces work from a distance? Select all the answers that are true.

a. An electric charge is strongest when it is farther away from the object.

b. Objects charged with static electricity repel or attract.

c. Sparks sometimes jump between a charged object and another object.

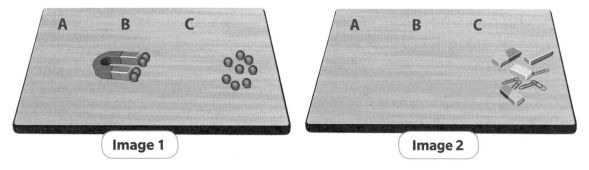

Image 1

Image 2

6. Look at the images above. Use the spaces below to draw the effect you would see for each statement.

Image 1: The magnet is moved to location A.

Image 2: A magnet is placed at location C.

Unit Review

Think about the forces acting on the pumpkin in the image.

1. Circle the words that describe the forces causing the pumpkin to move.
   a. push
   b. pull
   c. balanced forces
   d. unbalanced forces

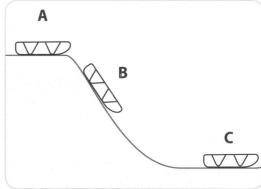

2. Predict the pattern of motion the wheels will show as the cart is pulled.
   a. back and forth
   b. up and down
   c. circular
   d. zigzag

Look at the sledding model. The sled is not moving at locations A and C.

3. At each location, draw and label arrows to show the forces that cause the sled to move or be still.

4. Choose a location. Describe how the forces you drew are affecting the sled at that location. Be sure to explain whether the forces are balanced or unbalanced.

_____

_____

_____

_____

_____

5. Cody is at a baseball game. The batter runs to first base and has to slide to be safe. How does friction affect the batter as he slides into first base?

6. Observe the cat in the photo. Which part of the cat's motion is predictable and which is not predictable?

7. Your friend swings a metal pendulum. Someone brings a magnet near the pendulum but does not touch it. Predict what will happen to the pattern of motion of the pendulum.

You build an electromagnet and test its strength using weights. The results of your investigation are shown below. Use this information to answer questions 8 and 9.

Weight (kg)	Lifted (yes/no)
1	yes
2	yes
4	no
8	no

8. Explain what causes the heavier weights to stay on the ground.

9. Ask a question that you can investigate based on this data. Write a plan to answer your question. Be sure your plan includes the one variable you will test and the number of times you will test the electromagnet.

10. Define a problem that can be solved using magnetic properties. Include one criterion and two constraints of a successful solution. Explain how your solution improves an existing technology.

In Unit 2, you conducted investigations to see patterns in how forces affect objects. In this unit, you will use patterns to make and use model life cycles of living things. You will explain how living things of the same type can be alike and different.

UNIT 3 Life Cycles and Inherited Traits

All Organisms Have a Life Cycle

There's something new!

What do you notice about the plant and the turtle?

I notice: _____

_____

_____

_____

What do you wonder about the ways the plant and turtle will change as they grow?

I wonder _____

_____

_____

_____

Can You Explain It?

How do you think both the plant and the turtle will change throughout their lives? Sketch, write, or model your answer.

Exploring a Change

Living things, like this bee and plant, are known as **organisms**. All organisms change as they get older. However, different organisms change in different ways.

Form a question Ask a question that you can study about how a seed changes over time.

Did you know?

The largest seed is the coco de mer, or sea coconut.

MATERIALS

- [ ] goggles
- [ ] non-latex gloves
- [ ] seed, 4 types
- [ ] plastic cup for planting seeds
- [ ] permanent marker
- [ ] graduated cylinder
- [ ] soil
- [ ] water
- [ ] ruler

STEP 1 **Investigate your question** Select a seed type. Get a cup and write your name on it with a permanent marker. Fill the cup ¾ full of soil. Put the seed 1 inch deep in the soil. Add water to moisten the soil. Place your cup next to a window.

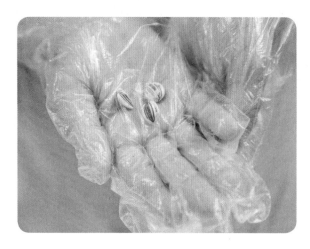

STEP 2 **Collect data** Each week, record the height of your plant and any other observations you make. Add water regularly to keep the soil moist.

STEP 3 **Organize your data** Create a data table to record your data.

STEP 4 **Analyze data** Compare your data with other groups. Identify any patterns you observe in your shared data.

 Turn to your neighbor and discuss anything about this investigation that was difficult and how you handled it.

Draw conclusions Make a claim to predict what would happen if you planted a different type of seed. Support your **claim** with **evidence** from your investigation, and explain your **reasoning.**

Making Sense

How does the data you gathered in this investigation help you begin to explain how the plant and turtle might change over time?

Comparing Life Cycles

These birds are at different stages of their **life cycles**, or changes that happen to an organism during its lifetime. Not all life cycles look the same.

Form a question Ask a question about the pattern of life cycles of different organisms.

Did you know?

The adult mayfly only lives for one day, but a red urchin can live for over 200 years!

STEP 1 **Make a plan** Pick a plant or a bird to research.

STEP 2 **Research** Find out about the changes your organism goes through.

STEP 3 **Develop a model** Make flashcards that show four changes. Come up with a name for each change.

STEP 4 **Share information** Share your flashcards with the class. What patterns do you see in the life cycles?

MATERIALS

☐ books

☐ colored pencils

☐ computer

☐ index cards

Make a **claim** about the similarities and differences of plant and animal life cycles. Support your claim with **evidence** from your investigation, and explain your **reasoning.**

Making Sense

How do your claim and evidence help you understand how the plant and turtle may change next?

So Many Changes!

It's a Dog's Life!

You have learned that organisms go through changes as they get older. All life cycles follow patterns that happen in a certain order. Look at the pictures of dogs in different life stages.

This puppy has just been born. Birth is the first stage in the life cycle of all animals.

This dog is near the end of its life cycle and will eventually die. Death is the end of a life cycle.

The adult dog has just completed the reproduction stage by having these puppies. Without reproduction, there would be no puppies.

This puppy is growing. Organisms grow during their lives. During this time, the puppy gets bigger and learns behaviors.

Use the word bank to put the life cycle in order.

| birth | death | growth | reproduction |

$\longrightarrow$ _____ $\longrightarrow$ _____ $\longrightarrow$ _____

Step by Step

A **population** is made up of all the members of a certain kind of organism in an environment. A population of emperor penguins works together to protect and raise hatchlings. Think about how the life cycle of a penguin differs from that of a dog.

Penguins are born when they hatch from eggs. From the time a penguin egg is laid, it must incubate for 32–68 days before it is ready to hatch.

During its growth stage, a young penguin will increase in size and weight. Adult feathers replace fuzzy down feathers.

Or

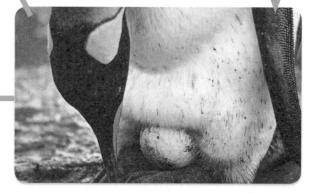

This is an older penguin. Many types of penguins can live for up to 20 years! But, eventually, all penguins die.

Penguins reproduce by laying eggs. Female penguins lay the eggs, and she and her mate protect it.

How is a life cycle a pattern?

Research another bird and draw or write its life cycle below. Be sure to label each stage.

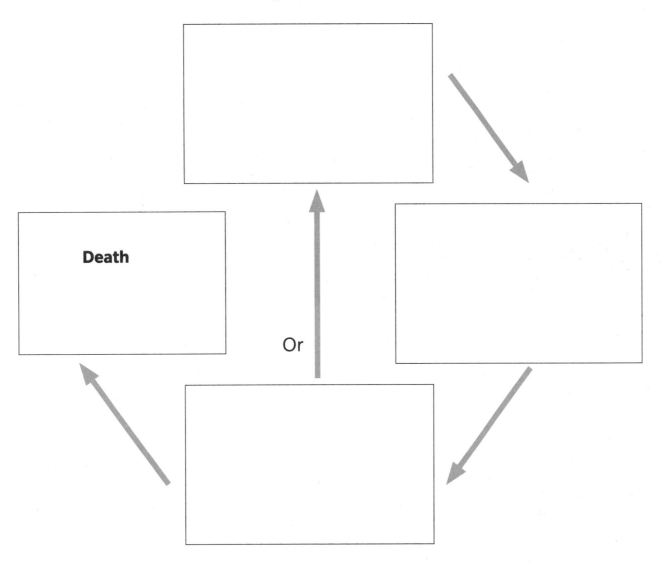

Draw conclusions Could the arrows in your drawing of a bird's life cycle go in the opposite direction? Make a **claim**. Use **evidence** to support your **reasoning**.

_____

_____

 Turn to your partner, and discuss a strategy you can use when giving feedback. Then, exchange your models and give each other feedback.

Flowers Galore

Flowering plants come in many varieties, but they all follow a similar life cycle. The life cycle of an apple tree is shown below.

Germination
During the first stage, a root begins to sprout from the seed.

Young tree
After the apple seed germinates, it grows into a young plant.

Adult tree
When the apple tree becomes an adult, it develops flowers.

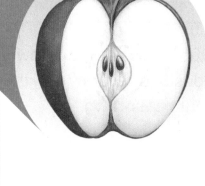

Reproduction
Pollinated flowers may turn into apples. The apples have seeds.

Seed
When the apple falls to the ground, the seeds can start a new life cycle.

Death
Apple trees may reproduce many times. In the end, the apple tree dies.

Write or draw each stage where it belongs in this model of an apple tree's life cycle.

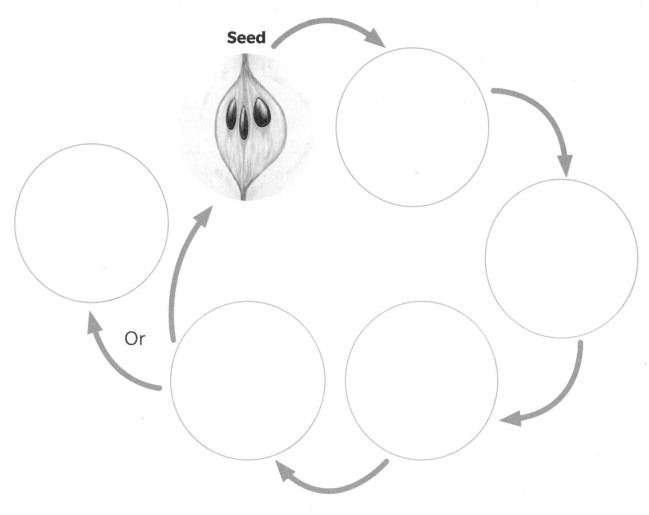

Seed

Or

Making Sense

How do the patterns you have observed help you understand the ways in which the plant and turtle go through similar changes?

_____

_____

How Do Life Cycles Differ?

Flowering and Nonflowering Plants

Flowering plants and nonflowering plants look different, but they have similar life cycles. Both plants make many seeds during reproduction, but they do it differently. Look at the life cycles of a flowering tomato plant and a nonflowering pine tree.

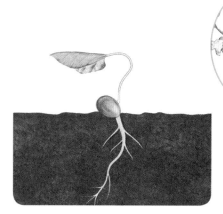

Like an apple plant, a tomato plant germinates from a seed.

A young tomato plant grows into an adult with flowers, which can turn into fruit.

germination   **growth**

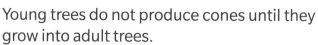

A new plant sprouts from a seed under the right conditions.

Young trees do not produce cones until they grow into adult trees.

How is the life cycle of a tomato plant different than the life cycle of a pine tree?

_____

_____

If a tomato falls to the ground, its seeds can start a new life cycle.

Death is the end of a tomato plant's life cycle.

reproduction   **death**

Seeds form inside cones rather than fruit.

A pine tree can live and reproduce for many years. Eventually, it will stop reproducing and die.

Insect Changes

Most insects go through a special change, called metamorphosis, during their life cycles. In *complete metamorphosis*, a young insect does not look like an adult. In *incomplete metamorphosis*, a young insect looks similar to an adult. Study the cicada and ladybug life cycles.

A cicada begins its life cycle when it hatches from an egg.

As a cicada grows, it becomes too large for its covering. When this happens it sheds its covering. This can occur many times.

birth   **growth**

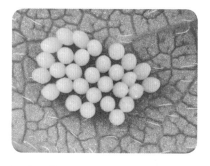

In its first stage, a ladybug hatches from an egg.

In the second stage of its life cycle, a ladybug is a worm-like larva. It eats a lot as it grows!

In the third stage, the larva makes a protective covering for itself and becomes a pupa.

Circle the insect that goes through complete metamorphosis.

cicada   ladybug

An adult cicada has wings and reproduces by laying eggs in holes made in branches.

The last stage of the cicada's life cycle is death. In the wild, a cicada can live up to 17 years.

reproduction　　　　　　　　**death**

When the ladybug comes out of the pupa, it can reproduce. It lays eggs underneath leaves.

This ladybug is nearing the end of its life and will eventually die. A ladybug in the wild can live up to three years.

Compare and contrast the life cycles of a cicada and a ladybug.

What About Amphibians?

Amphibians are animals that live part of their lives in the water and part of their lives on land. Salamanders and frogs are both amphibians. Using patterns in the salamander life cycle, predict the life cycle of a frog, and fill in the timeline.

Salamander

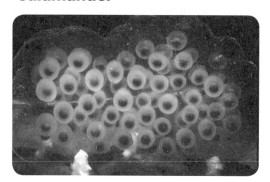

A salamander hatches from an egg during its birth stage.

A young salamander lives in water. When it develops full legs and lungs, it leaves the water to live on land.

birth

growth

Frog

When it is ready to reproduce, an adult salamander returns to the water in order to lay eggs.

Eventually, the salamander dies.

reproduction

death

Making Sense

How does your understanding of the life cycles of different organisms help you explain why the life cycles of the plant and turtle are different?

_____

_____

_____

Broken Cycles

What If?

Life cycles can be interrupted for many reasons. Some interruptions happen naturally because of predators or severe weather. Human actions can also disrupt life cycles.

Seeds are made when bees carry pollen from one flower to another. What happens to the plants if bees stop visiting the flowers?

_____

_____

_____

An adult female turtle recently laid her eggs. However, a snake found her nest and ate the eggs. Predict what will happen to the turtle population if this happens to other turtle eggs.

_____

Too much or too little water can affect a plant's life cycle. Predict what happens to the life cycles of plants during a drought.

_____

_____

_____

Clearing land to make room for buildings can disrupt plant and animal life cycles. Predict whether plant or animal life cycles are most affected in this area.

_____

_____

_____

Pollution can damage plants with harmful chemicals in the air or water. How might polluted air or water affect a plant's life cycle?

_____

_____

_____

Death Defying

You know that the end of any animal's life cycle is death. What would happen if no animals in a bear population died?

Complete the table to find out.

Year	Adult	Young	Offspring population
2020	10	× 2	
2025	30	× 2	
2030	90	× 2	

Using patterns found in the table, predict what would happen to the bear population by the year 2040.

If the pattern continues, predict what will happen to the populations of organisms that the bears eat.

Making Sense

How does your understanding of interrupted life cycles affect your understanding of how the plant and turtle will change during their lives?

Lesson Check

Can You Explain It?

Review your ideas from the beginning of this lesson about how a plant and turtle will change throughout their lives. How have your ideas changed? Be sure to do the following:

- Identify the stages of each organism's life cycle.
- Describe how life cycles are unique and diverse.
- Explain the importance of reproduction.

Now I know or think that _____

_____

_____

Making Connections

This adult salamander hatches from eggs. How is its life cycle like the plant and turtle at the beginning of the lesson? How is it different?

_____

_____

_____

_____

Checkpoints

1. Complete the life cycle model. Label the pattern of life cycle stages that all organisms go through.

_____   _____   _____

2. Order the pattern of a flowering plant's life cycle below, 1–6. Then match each stage with its description.

Order	Stage	Description
_____	reproduction	end of a plant's life cycle
_____	young adult	roots sprout from a seed
_____	seed	plant quickly grows taller
_____	germination	start of a new life cycle
_____	death	plant forms flowers
_____	adult	plant forms fruit

3. All life cycles have a predictable pattern, but are not exactly alike. Compare and contrast two life cycles that are different.

_____

_____

_____

_____

4. A fox eats a young mole. Draw a model to show the pattern of the mole's interrupted life cycle.

5. Explain why reproduction is important for all organisms.

6. A bee keeper has 25 bee hives. He notices that some of the hives are dying. His neighbor owns an orange grove that is pollinated by the bees. Look at the table below. Predict the number of crates of oranges the tree will produce in year 4 if the pattern continues.

Year	# of beehives	# of crates of oranges
1	25	100
2	20	80
3	15	60
4	10	

Plants and Animals Inherit Traits from Their Parents

Look at all those little chicks!

What do you notice about these chicks?

I notice: _____

_____

_____

What do you wonder about these chicks?

I wonder: _____

_____

_____

Can You Explain It?

Why do these chicks look similar to, yet different from, their parents and each other? Sketch, write, or model your answer.

What Will It Look Like?

When organisms reproduce, the young are called **offspring**. You may be able to match parent animals with their offspring by looking at their **traits**. Traits are features that are passed down from parents to their offspring.

Form a question Ask a question about how offspring look similar to their parents.

Did you know?

Some features in offspring are more likely to be seen than others.

Look at the images below. Use what you know about traits to decide which calves are most likely the offspring of the Texas Longhorn parents. Circle all that apply.

Male parent

Female parent

Select one of the offspring and make a **claim** about which characteristics it got from each parent. Support your claim with **evidence** from the images. Explain your **reasoning**.

_____

_____

Making Sense

How does this activity help you understand why the chicks look similar to the parent in the image?

_____

_____

© Houghton Mifflin Harcourt Publishing Company • Image Credits: (tl) ©James Laurie/Shutterstock; (tr) ©Ivo Roospold/Alamy; (bl) ©Tim McCaig/Getty Images; (bcl) ©Thorsten Scholz/EyeEm/Getty Images; (bcr) ©TFoxFoto/Shutterstock; (br) ©with-God/Shutterstock

Monster Traits

Parents pass traits down to their offspring. Siblings may inherit different information from each parent, making them look different from one another.

Form a question Ask a question about traits that you will investigate.

Did you know?

Each parent gives some of its traits to its offspring.

_____

_____

MATERIALS

- ☐ monster parent traits table
- ☐ coins
- ☐ Monster Trait Handout Sheets (2)
- ☐ crayons or colored pencils
- ☐ scissors
- ☐ glue

STEP 1   **Investigate your question** Flip two coins to determine which traits your offspring monster inherits from each parent.

STEP 2   **Organize your data** Use your results to find the inherited trait in the table below. Repeat this for each trait, and then complete the table.

Monster Parent Traits				
Body part	Mother (2 heads)	Father (2 tails)	Blended (1 heads, 1 tails)	Offspring
Arms	6	4	5	
Face	square	round	try again	
Eyes	3	1	2	
Mouth	lots of big square teeth	3 sharp teeth	3 square teeth	
Hair style	lots of curly hair	short, spiky hair	short, curly hair	
Hair color	green	purple	try again	

STEP 3   **Develop a model** Cut out the traits your monster inherited from its parents. Glue your offspring monster together. Don't forget to color and decorate your monster.

STEP 4 **Analyze your data** Compare your monster with other monsters in the class. Identify patterns in how they look. How and why are they similar and different?

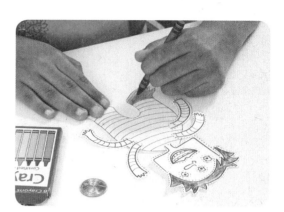

 Turn to a partner and discuss ways to help someone who feels like they don't fit in to feel welcome.

Make a **claim** about inherited traits based on what you observed. Cite **evidence** to support your claim, and explain your **reasoning**.

Making Sense

How does this investigation help you understand why chicks that don't look alike could still be siblings?

Parents and Offspring

Family Tree

You can look at parents and their offspring to see some of the traits that have been passed down. Use the similarities and differences in the traits of the flowers below to draw the missing parent or offspring.

Parent 1   **Parent 2**   **Offspring**

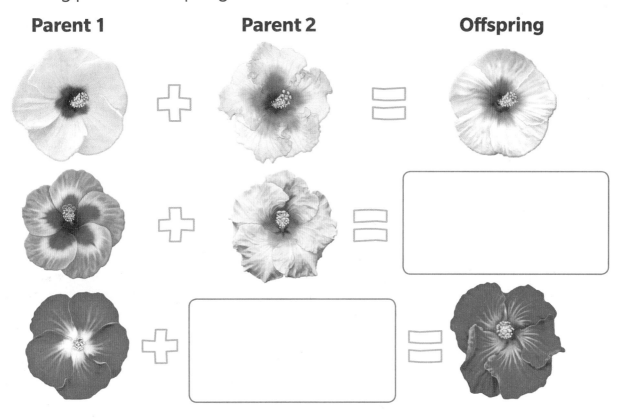

 Discuss with a partner how someone who has a difficult time drawing could answer the above question without becoming frustrated.

What patterns of traits did you consider when drawing the missing flowers?

Similar But Not Related

Some animals look similar. For example, these birds both have beaks and wings. The color of their feathers is also similar. But when you compare them more closely, each of these traits is different.

This hawk has a large, sharp beak. It eats small animals. It also has large, strong wings to soar, hunt, and catch prey.

....

This sparrow has a small beak. It eats insects and seeds. It also has small, narrow wings to quickly fly from branch to branch.

....

Birds of prey, such as a hawk, are birds that hunt and eat animals that are close to their own size. Use the data in the table below as evidence to determine if each bird is a bird of prey.

Birds of a Feather?				
Bird	**Beak size**	**Wings**	**Diet**	**Birds of prey**
owl	large	large	mice	
cardinal	small	small	berries	
snow bunting	small	small	seeds	
falcon	large	large	small birds	

● ● ●

Making Sense

How does your understanding of traits help you explain why the chicks resemble their parents but are not identical to them?

_____

_____

© Houghton Mifflin Harcourt Publishing Company • Image Credits: (l) ©Chris Hill/Shutterstock; (r) ©All Canada Photos/Michelle Valberg/Alamy

Lesson Check

Can You Explain It?

Review your ideas from the beginning of this lesson about why these chicks look similar, but not identical, to their parents and each other. How have your ideas changed? Be sure to do the following:

- Discuss the traits you observe.
- Identify where traits come from.
- Explain why the chicks look different.

Now I know or think that _____ .

_____

_____

Making Connections

This is a field that has all the same flowers. Some of the flowers are different colors. How is this like the chicken and chicks at the beginning of the lesson? How is it different?

_____

_____

_____

Checkpoints

1. Observe the photo of the dogs. If they reproduced, what traits would you predict their offspring would have in common? Cite evidence to support your reasoning.

_____

_____

_____

2. A female elk gives birth to an offspring. What would you expect the offspring to look like? Circle the best answer.

a. The offspring would look exactly like its mother because it inherits all traits from its mother.

b. The offspring would look exactly like its father because it inherits all traits from its father.

c. The offspring would look similar to both the mother and the father because it inherits traits from both parents.

d. The offspring would not look like either parent because it inherits traits from its siblings.

3. Some animals inherit sharp teeth so that they can eat meat. Other animals inherit flat teeth so that they can eat plants. Using this pattern, classify each animal in the table as one that eats animals or plants.

Animal	Type of teeth	Food (animal/plant)
tiger	sharp	
horse	flat	
cow	flat	
coyote	sharp	

Offspring

Parents

4. Observe the photos above. Draw a line from each offspring to its parents. What patterns did you use to match each offspring to its parent?

_____

_____

5. Complete the table below to compare the traits of the two pea plants.

Trait	Pea plants	
leaf shape	same	different
leaf color	same	different
petal color	same	different
height	same	different
overall shape	same	different

6. Use the data in the table to explain whether or not these plants are siblings.

_____

_____

Organisms Use Strategies to Be Successful in Their Environment

These guys stay between the lines!

What do you notice about these zebras?

I notice _____

_____

_____

What do you wonder about these zebras?

I wonder _____

_____

_____

Can You Explain It?

What advantages do these zebras have for surviving in their environment? Sketch, write, or model your answer.

Battle of the Beans!

Do you see the moth in the photo above? Why do you think it is so hard to find? The moth's markings blend in with its surroundings. This is called *camouflage*. This helps the moth survive.

Form a question What questions do you have about how camouflage helps an organism survive?

Did you know?

There are over 150,000 different species of moth in the world!

MATERIALS

- ☐ 30 dry white beans
- ☐ 30 dry black beans
- ☐ cup
- ☐ white paper
- ☐ black paper
- ☐ patterned paper
- ☐ timer

STEP 1 **Investigate your question** Working with a partner, place the black paper on the table. Randomly scatter beans over the paper.

One partner will keep time. The other will close their eyes, open them, pick up the first bean they see, and set it aside. Continue this for 15 seconds. Record the number of white beans still on the paper in the table below. Replace the beans, and do this again.

Trade roles and do two more trials.

STEP 2 **Organize your data** Record the number of each bean that is still on the paper after each turn.

Paper	Trial 1		Trial 2	
	Partner A	**Partner B**	**Partner A**	**Partner B**
White				
Black				
Patterned paper				

STEP 3   Repeat Step 1 using the white paper, and then repeat again using the patterned paper.

   Turn to your partner and discuss any problems you had completing the activity.

STEP 4   **Analyze your data** Look for patterns in your data. Explain how the color of the paper affected which beans you picked up.

Compare your data to another group's data. Make a **claim** about how body color affects the way animals are able to survive in their environment. Cite your **evidence,** and explain your **reasoning.**

Making Sense

How does the evidence you gathered in this investigation help you explain how a zebra's stripes help it survive in its environment?

All for One

Have you ever heard the phrase "strength in numbers"? Wolves live in groups called *packs*. A pack usually has about six wolves. This helps them survive in different ways.

Form a question What question do you have about how living in large groups help animals survive?

Did you know?

A group of zebras is called a dazzle.

STEP 1 **Investigate your question** Using the table below, place the number of each marble into a bag. Pick one marble out of the bag. Record its color below.

MATERIALS

☐ 1 red marble

☐ 13 blue marbles

☐ paper bag

# of red	# of blue	Color drawn		
		Trial 1	**Trial 2**	**Trial 3**
1	1			
1	3			
1	5			
1	9			
1	13			

STEP 2 **Draw conclusions** Look for patterns in your data. Share your data with your class. Discuss the cause of these patterns.

Make a **claim** about how the total number of marbles affects the chance of picking the red marble. Support your claim with **evidence** from your investigation and explain your **reasoning.**

Making Sense

How does your claim and the evidence you gathered in this investigation help you understand the benefit of zebras living in a dazzle?

© Houghton Mifflin Harcourt Publishing Company • Image Credits: ©Houghton Mifflin Harcourt

Differences That Win

Characteristics for Survival

Animals and plants have many characteristics that help them survive and reproduce. This pitcher plant grows in soil that does not have a lot of nutrients. To survive, it gets its nutrients from insects, such as flies. Because the plant can't move to get the flies, it has specialized characteristics to help it trap the insects.

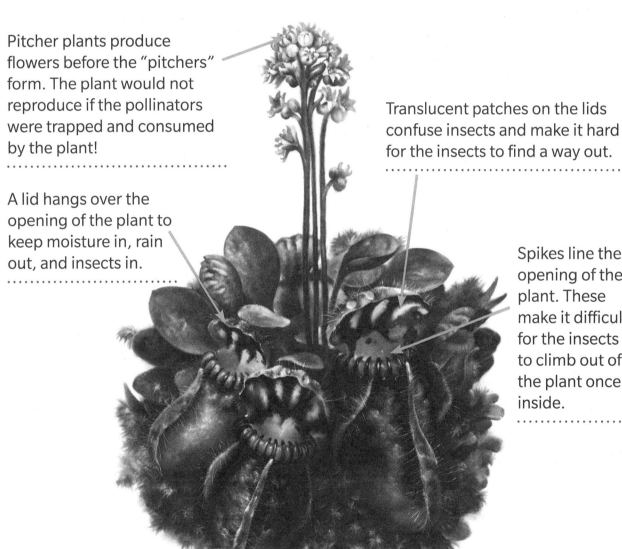

Pitcher plants produce flowers before the "pitchers" form. The plant would not reproduce if the pollinators were trapped and consumed by the plant!

Translucent patches on the lids confuse insects and make it hard for the insects to find a way out.

A lid hangs over the opening of the plant to keep moisture in, rain out, and insects in.

Spikes line the opening of the plant. These make it difficult for the insects to climb out of the plant once inside.

Traits That Make It

Differences in traits can be helpful or harmful. Traits that help organisms survive in their environment are important. Organisms that survive longer can reproduce more times.

Tan jaguars are larger and live on grasslands. Their tan color and spots make it easier for them to blend in with the grassland.

Black jaguars are usually smaller and live in trees. Their black color makes them harder to see in the shadows.

Some traits, like the ones in the sparrows below, can affect the chances of an organism to find a mate and reproduce.

The white-striped sparrow is easier to see, so it is usually more aggressive. Male sparrows prefer females with white stripes because they defend their home and young.

Tan-striped males are usually more hidden. They are less likely to be involved in fighting and often help more with raising offspring.

A hummingbird has a long, thin, curved beak. This helps it reach the nectar inside long and hollow flowers that other birds cannot reach. As they do this, they spread pollen from flower to flower. How would the offspring of this hummingbird be affected if it had a shorter beak?

The seeds of dandelions are attached to bristles that act like a parachute, which helps them travel in the wind. How would the travel of dandelion seeds be affected by the size of the bristles?

Select a photo above. How might variations in that trait affect the population over time?

_____

_____

Making Sense

How does this exploration help you understand better how the traits of the zebras help them survive in their environment?

_____

_____

Better Together

Safety in Numbers!

Many animals, such as dolphins and elephants, live in groups. The structures below are coral. Some people think coral are rocks or ocean plants. But coral are actually many tiny animals that live together in a group. As they grow together, they form coral reefs.

Coral is made up of tiny organisms.

What do you think are some advantages of animals living in large groups?

Living as part of a group can help animals survive. Look at the examples below to learn how living in groups is helpful.

Antelope travel in large herds. The coloring of an antelope's fur makes it hard for predators to focus on a single antelope when they run together.

These leaf-cutter ants have different jobs, such as weaving nests, hunting for food, and laying eggs.

A group of hyenas is called a *clan*. A clan usually includes about 40 to 80 members. A clan can hunt and take down larger animals by working together.

 The ants in a colony all have roles. Turn and talk to a partner about how having roles helps you complete an investigation.

What do you think would happen if one of the organisms above ended up alone?

Living as part of a group can help animals protect their young. And groups can work together to cope with changes in the environment.

To protect their offspring, sperm whales work together to raise their young. With better protection, more young reach adulthood.

Coping with the harsh cold of winter, male penguins huddle together. This behavior keeps their eggs warmer.

How might a warmer climate affect the behavior of the penguin group?

Making Sense

How does your understanding of living in groups help you explain why zebras live in dazzles?

Lesson Check

Can You Explain It?

Review your ideas from the beginning of this lesson about how zebras are able to survive.

Be sure to do the following:

- Describe traits that help keep zebras safe.
- Explain how living in groups helps the zebras.

Now I know or think that _____

_____

_____

_____

_____

Making Connections

Some types of fish travel in groups called *schools*. How is this like the zebras living in harems? How is it different?

_____

_____

_____

Checkpoints

1. What helpful effect does traveling in a group have on these dolphins?

    a. They are hidden from predators.

    b. They can swim slower.

    c. They can better care for their young.

    d. They can better hunt sharks.

2. A pack of wolves is much smaller than a colony of penguins. How would traveling in larger groups affect wolves?

3. A group of lions is called a *pride*. Write a cause-and-effect statement about a benefit of living in a pride. What evidence would support your statement?

4. Use the table to answer the question.

Explain how the size of the thorns on each plant affects the survival of those plants.

Thorn size	# of plants eaten
small	12
medium	7
large	2

_____

_____

Use the information below to answer the questions.

Male bowerbirds build nests to attract a mate for reproduction. Female bowerbirds like nests with lots of decorations.

5. What effect does the ability to build a good nest have on a male bowerbird's ability to reproduce?

_____

_____

6. What might happen to a male bowerbird that can't build a good nest?

_____

_____

Unit Review

1. All organisms go through similar stages in their life cycles. Which stage makes a life cycle a pattern? Circle and then explain your answer.

a. birth   **b.** growth   **c.** reproduction   **d.** death

2. Look at the data in the table. Then, answer the question.

Animal	Length of life
One hyena living in a group	12 years
One hyena living alone	1 year
One black garden ant living in a group	15 years
One black garden ant living alone	2 weeks

What causes the changes in the life span for each kind of organism?

3. The image on the left shows two adult moose. Observe the images on the right and circle the animal that should also be classified as a moose.

A   B   C

© Houghton Mifflin Harcourt Publishing Company • Image Credits: (bl) ©Keith Szafranski/Getty Images; (bcl) ©twildlife/Getty Images; (bcr) ©Snap2Art_RF/Getty Images; (br) ©Colleen Gara/Getty Images;

4. What features of the animals did you use to classify them as a moose or not a moose in question 3?

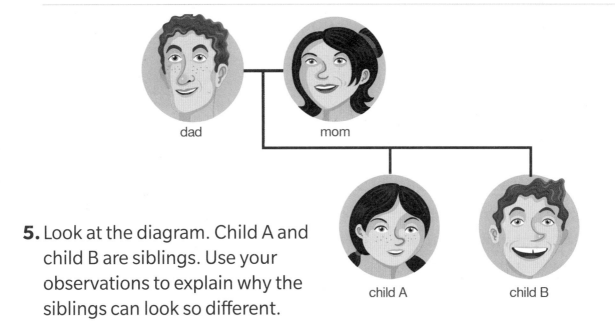

dad

mom

child A

child B

5. Look at the diagram. Child A and child B are siblings. Use your observations to explain why the siblings can look so different.

6. Make a claim about how a third sibling might look different from the two shown. Describe the traits they might have and use evidence from the images to argue for your claim.

7. Form an argument about the chances for survival of a zebra without stripes compared to a zebra with stripes. Use evidence from the unit to support your argument.

Look at the image. Use your observations to answer questions 8 and 9.

8. Use your knowledge of life cycle patterns to predict the possible stages that the adult plant may go through next. Circle all that apply.

  a. germination   **c.** reproduction

  b. growth   **d.** death

9. Use what you know about patterns in plant life cycles to make a model of this plant's life cycle. Write your answer or draw a model on a separate piece of paper.

10. Explain how the stages in the life cycle of a plant are similar to the stages in a cat's life cycle.

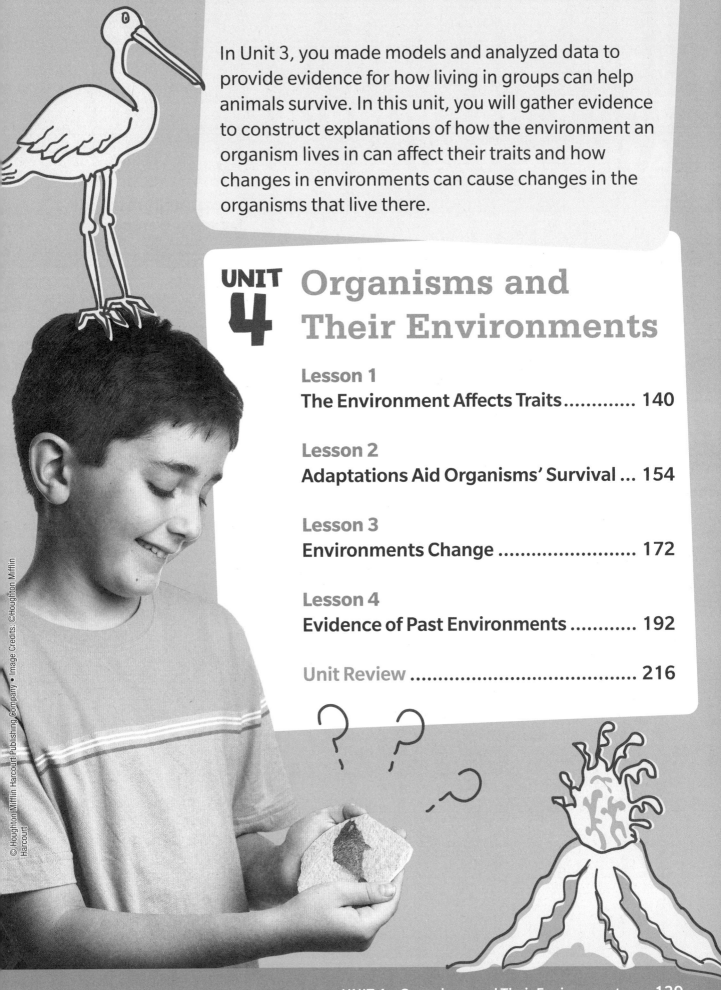

In Unit 3, you made models and analyzed data to provide evidence for how living in groups can help animals survive. In this unit, you will gather evidence to construct explanations of how the environment an organism lives in can affect their traits and how changes in environments can cause changes in the organisms that live there.

UNIT 4 Organisms and Their Environments

© Houghton Mifflin Harcourt Publishing Company • Image Credits: ©Houghton Mifflin Harcourt

The Environment Affects Traits

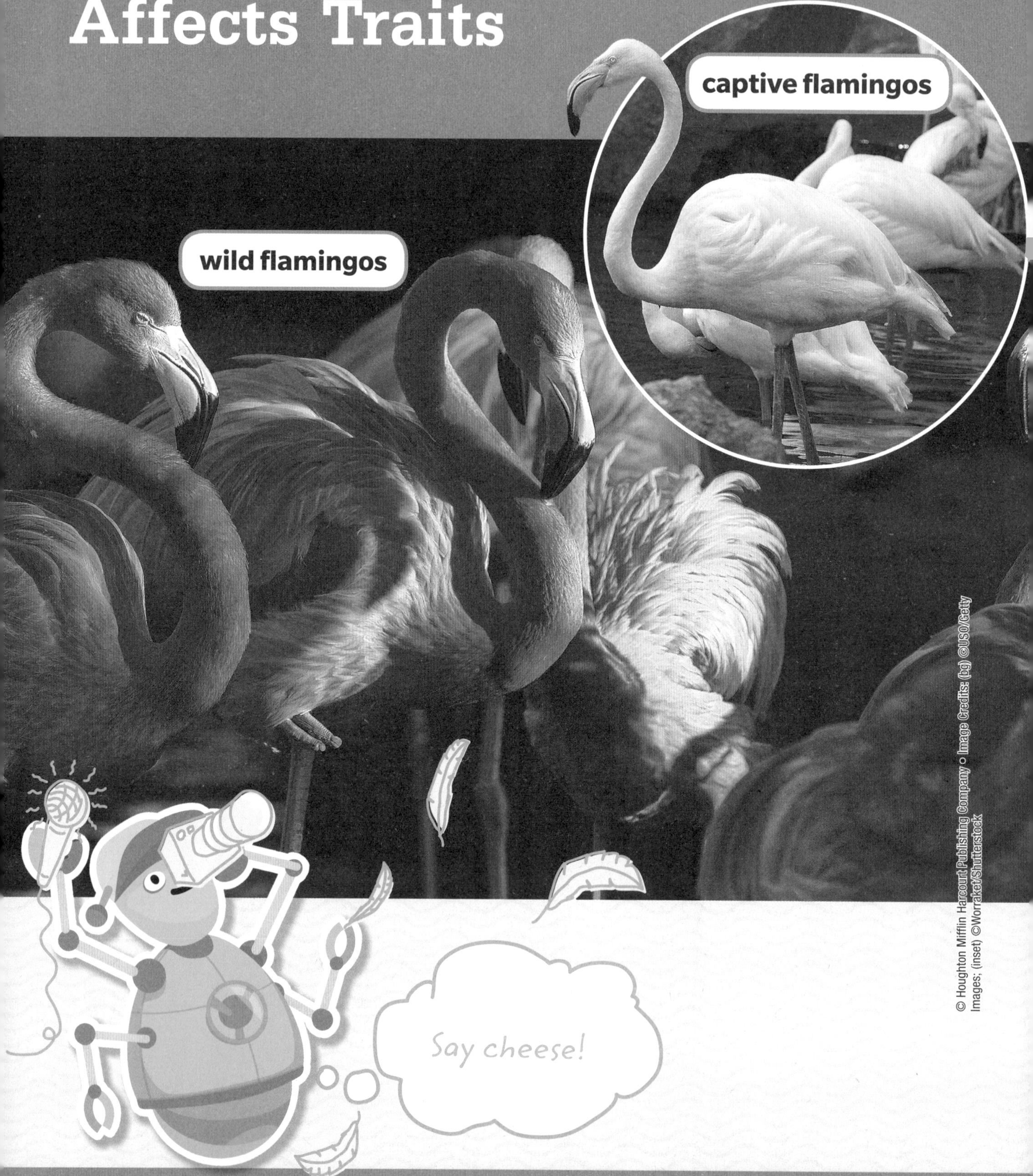

captive flamingos

wild flamingos

Say cheese!

What do you notice about these flamingos?

I notice _____

_____

_____

What do you wonder about these flamingos?

I wonder _____

_____

_____

Can You Explain It?

What do you think causes these flamingos to look
different from each other? Sketch, write, or model
your answer.

Will They Grow?

Organisms are affected by their **environments**, or all the living and nonliving things around it. Seeds require certain conditions to germinate.

Form a question Ask a question that you can investigate about how environments can affect plants.

> **Did you know?**
>
> A drought-tolerant plant is a plant that can survive on very little water.

© Houghton Mifflin Harcourt Publishing Company • Image Credits: ©Tony Rolls/Alamy

POSSIBLE MATERIALS

- [ ] lima bean
- [ ] paper towel, damp
- [ ] permanent marker
- [ ] soil
- [ ] plastic zip bag

STEP 1 **Make a plan** Select an environmental condition—wet or dry—to investigate. Write it in the space below.

STEP 2 **Investigate your question** Wrap one lima bean in a damp paper towel or a dry paper towel, and place it in a plastic zip bag. Write your name on the bag with a permanent marker.

STEP 3 **Organize data** Decide what data you will collect. Observe your bean every few days. Make a data table and record your results in the space below.

STEP 4 **Analyze data** Compare your results with the rest of the class. Then, write a cause-and-effect statement that summarizes your findings.

Make a **claim** about how the environment you selected affected the growth of the lima bean plant. Support your claim with **evidence** from your investigation and explain your **reasoning**.

Making Sense

How does the evidence you gathered in this investigation help you begin to understand the cause-and-effect relationship between the two groups of flamingos and their environments?

© Houghton Mifflin Harcourt Publishing Company • Image Credits: ©Houghton Mifflin Harcourt

Designed Environments

A chameleon may change color as it interacts with its environment. This helps it stay hidden.

Form a question Ask a question about the relationship between an organism that can change color, such as a chameleon or an octopus, and its environment.

Did you know?

Some kinds of chameleons can turn blue!

STEP 1	**Research** Learn about chameleon behaviors.

MATERIALS

- ☐ books
- ☐ colored pencils
- ☐ computer
- ☐ index cards

STEP 2	**Develop a model** Design an environment in which a chameleon could survive well. Sketch it on a piece of paper.

STEP 3	Share your design with a partner. Discuss the differences in your designs and explain how they might affect the chameleon.

 Different environments affect people, too. Talk with a partner about how you act at home versus somewhere new. Listen respectfully to each other.

Make a **claim** about how a chameleon in a jungle would be different from one living in a designed environment made of wood and soil. Use **evidence** and **reasoning** to support your claim.

Making Sense

How does knowing the ways that natural and designed environments can affect the chameleon help you understand the difference in the flamingos' colors?

Plants and Their Environments

Environmental Factors

Factors in the environment may affect plant structures or traits. Plants are affected by the amount of water, light, and nutrients they receive.

The amount of water a plant receives can affect its growth. This plant received too much water.

Too much light has caused this leaf to turn brown.

Sometimes nutrients in soil affect the color of flowers. The amount of certain nutrients in the soil cause these plants to grow flowers in very different colors.

The color of these hydrangeas is affected by the nutrients in the soil where they grow.

People or animals can change plants when they cut off or eat part of it. Cutting some plants keeps them small, but cutting other plants makes them grow back bushier.

Trimming, or pruning, basil promotes plant growth. Regularly pruning the basil plant helps it to grow back taller and bushier. This results in more basil.

 Think of one way you are affected by your environment. Explain how you are affected and how that makes you feel.

Making Sense

How does your understanding of how the environment affects plants help you begin to understand why the flamingos look so different?

Animals and Their Environments

Can the Environment Affect Animal Features?

You have learned that factors in the environment may affect the features and traits of plants. Some factors may also affect traits of animals. These factors may include temperature and nutrients.

Temperature determines gender in many reptiles. Alligator eggs developed at a warmer temperature produce males. In turtles, warm temperatures produce females.

This sea slug is brighter than others of the same type. Nutrients in the food it eats cause this to happen.

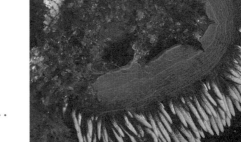

Compare and contrast how the environment affects hydrangeas and the sea slug above.

Look at the two photos of an Arctic fox below. One photo shows an Arctic fox during the summer and the other during the winter.

In the photos of the Arctic foxes, which trait varies throughout the year? Explain why time of year affects that trait.

Write a cause-and-effect statement about the amount of food and exercise that the cat in the photo gets.

Making Sense

How does knowing that environmental factors can affect the traits of animals help you explain why some of the flamingos are different shades of pink?

Lesson Check

Can You Explain It?

Review your ideas from the beginning of this lesson about the flamingos' colors. How have your ideas changed?

Be sure to do the following:

- Describe how the flamingos are similar.
- Identify the factors that make the groups of flamingos look different.

Now I know or think that _____

_____

_____

Making Connections

This walking stick can change its color and is often found in areas with a lot of trees. How are the effects of environmental factors similar for the flamingos and walking stick? How are they different?

_____

_____

Checkpoints

1. Turtles are reptiles. What is the most likely reason that your friend's turtle is a male? Circle your answer.

   a. The mother turtle had more nutrients.

   b. The egg developed at a certain temperature.

   c. The turtle was raised by its mother, not by its father.

   d. The egg developed in very dry soil.

2. Joni observes an indoor plant and notices that it has brown spots on its leaves. Explain what may have caused the plant to look this way and what could be done to prevent more spots from forming.

3. What effect does the arctic fox's ability to change colors have on the animals it hunts for food?

   a. The animals can hide more easily.

   b. The animals can spot the foxes more easily.

   c. The animals are more likely to be surprised and caught.

   d. The animals will no longer be hunted by the foxes.

4. A science class grows lima beans in different environments. One student grows a bean in a dry environment, one student puts very little water on the paper towel, and one student uses a wet paper towel. The amount the lima bean sprouts grow each day is shown below, in inches.

Student	Environment	Day 1	Day 3	Day 5
Sally	A	3	5	7
Brendon	B	1	2	3
Julie	C	0	0	0

Describe the environment that Julie likely grew her lima bean in. Cite evidence for your reasoning.

5. Describe the environmental factors that resulted in this rat's appearance. What can the owners do to make the mouse healthier?

6. When cardinals eat berries from a dogwood tree, their feathers turn a brighter red. Explain why this happens.

Adaptations Aid Organisms' Survival

Hey! Where did you go?

What do you notice about this octopus?

I notice _____

_____

_____

_____

What do you wonder about this octopus?

I wonder _____

_____

_____

_____

Can You Explain It?

How do you think the look and behavior of this octopus
aids in its survival? Sketch, write, or model your answer.

How Do Structures Help?

skin

blubber

muscle

This leopard seal has blubber, or a thick layer of fat, under its skin. Many animals that live in cold environments have blubber to help keep them warm and store energy. All organisms have structures that help them survive in their environments.

Form a question   Ask a question that you can investigate about how an animal's physical structures help it survive in its environment.

Did you know?

Blubber helps a hippo float in water in spite of its large size.

STEP 1	**Investigate your question** Put a glove on one hand and submerge the gloved hand in an ice bath for 10 seconds. Remove your glove and throw it away.

POSSIBLE MATERIALS

- ☐ gloves (2)
- ☐ vegetable shortening
- ☐ thermometer, small
- ☐ ice bath
- ☐ plastic bags (2)
- ☐ goggles
- ☐ apron

STEP 2	**Collect data** Place a new glove on your hand. Cover it in a thick layer of vegetable shortening and submerge it in the ice bath for 10 seconds. Remove your glove and throw it away. Make a data table below and record your observations.

STEP 3	Place a thermometer in a plastic bag and submerge it in the ice bath for 10 seconds. Record your data in the data table.

STEP 4	Place the thermometer in a new bag. Cover the bag in shortening and submerge it in the ice bath for 10 seconds. Record your data in the data table.

STEP 5 **Draw conclusions** Examine the data for patterns. What do the patterns tell you about the effect of blubber?

Sharing results in groups can be difficult. What could you do to help someone who has results that are different from the rest of the class? Discuss your answer with a neighbor.

Make a **claim** about how the physical features of an organism relate to its environment. Share your claim with another group. Use your **evidence** and **reasoning** to support your argument to the other group.

Making Sense

How does understanding the way blubber helps a seal stay warm help you explain the importance of the octopus's ability to change color and shape?

© Houghton Mifflin Harcourt Publishing Company • Image Credits: ©Houghton Mifflin Harcourt

How Do Behaviors Help?

Animals also use certain behaviors to help them survive in their environment. Some animals hibernate when food is not readily available. During hibernation, animals are not active so they do not need much food.

Form a question Ask a question about how certain behaviors help animals survive in their environments.

© Houghton Mifflin Harcourt Publishing Company • Image Credits: ©Nature Picture Library/Ingo Arndt/Alamy

Did you know?

Brown bears usually hibernate from three to seven months in the wild.

STEP 1 **Make a plan** Pick a plant or animal you are interested in. Write it below.

STEP 2 **Research** Identify one or two behavioral strategies your organism uses to survive in its environment.

POSSIBLE MATERIALS

- ☐ books
- ☐ colored pencils
- ☐ Internet
- ☐ index cards

Neat!

Make a **claim** about how behaviors help organisms survive. Support your claim with **evidence** from your investigation and explain your **reasoning**.

Making Sense

How does understanding how the behavioral adaptations of animals in relation to their environment help you explain the behavior of the octopus?

Adapted Organisms

Berry Interesting!

Blackberry bushes can survive in many different environments. This is because they have many adaptations. An **adaptation** is a trait or characteristic that helps an organism survive.

Read the table below. Fill in the missing benefit to the blackberry bush.

Trait	Benefit
The leaves and stems grow back quickly, even after severe weather.	This allows the bush to survive in harsh conditions.
When an animal eats a berry, the berry seeds are scattered after passing through the animal.	This helps the blackberry bush reproduce in new areas.
Blackberry branches have very sharp thorns.	

Armadillo lizards live in the desert of South Africa, often living in the spaces between rocks. They are about 13 cm (5 in.) in length and move slowly. Like an armadillo, this lizard can curl into a ball when it feels threatened. It does this by lying on its back and biting its tail.

Complete the activity below to identify the cause-and-effect relationship between the armadillo lizard's adaptations and its environment.

Draw a line from the trait to the benefit that it provides.

Trait	Benefit
Sharp claws	discourages predators from eating it
Strong jaw	grip rocky surfaces
Spiny covering	used to attack when threatened and when defending its territory

There is a relationship between an organism and its **habitat.** A habitat provides all the needs for an organism's survival. It is the physical place where an organism lives in its environment. An organism's structures and behaviors help it survive in its habitat. For example, a sparrow has clawed feet that are adapted for gripping small tree branches. A duck, however, has webbed feet that help it swim in the water.

Parrots have strong wings because they need to be able to fly from tree to tree to find food in their jungle habitat.

Emus are birds that have small wings and strong legs. They run quickly in their habitat because they can't fly.

Vampire fish live in rivers in South America. They have a mouth full of very sharp teeth to catch the smaller fish that make up their diet.

Look at the teeth of this wild goat. Wild goat teeth are flat for grinding up the plants it eats in its habitat.

You meet some of your needs as well. Select one and write it below. Respectfully discuss with a classmate how you meet that need.

On Their Best Behavior

Physical characteristics are not the only adaptations that help animals survive. Animals also have behavioral adaptations that help them survive.

Naked mole rats live in narrow tunnels. Sometimes predators get in the tunnels. So naked mole rats can run as fast backward as they can forward!

Lizards can't warm or cool themselves. At night, their body temperature drops in the night air. In the morning, they find a patch of sunlight to warm up in.

Some animals in the same habitat help each other. This frog and tarantula don't seem like typical neighbors. But the frog eats ants that prey on the spider's eggs. The spider protects the frog from dangerous predators.

Making Sense

How does understanding the relationship between an organism and its habitat help you understand the need for the octopus's structures and behavior?

© Houghton Mifflin Harcourt Publishing Company • Image Credits: (tl) ©Raymond Mendez/Animals Animals/Earth Scenes; (cr) Corbis; (bl) ©FLPA/Alamy

Adaptation and Environment

Survival of the Fittest

There is a relationship between an organism and its habitat. A habitat provides the needs for an organism's survival. An organism's structures and behaviors make it successful in its habitat. A hippopotamus has several adaptations that help it survive in a warm, watery habitat.

A hippo's eyes, nose, and ears are on top of its head. This means the hippopotamus can spend most of its day almost completely underwater where it stays cool, breathes, and watches out for threats. When hippos go on land, they make a red liquid that protects their skin from the sun.

Would a hippopotamus survive well in a desert? Discuss your answer with a partner, and use evidence to support your argument.

Fun Ways to Fit In

Organisms have many different kinds of adaptations. Both physical and behavioral adaptations may protect an organism from predators or help it reproduce.

When opossums become very scared, they pretend to be dead and give off a smelly odor. This makes predators think that the opossum is decomposing.

The sweet pinesap grows under oak and pine trees. Its flowers are protected from animals by camouflage, or blending in, with dead leaves.

Monarch butterflies are poisonous to many animals. Viceroy butterflies are not. Viceroys mimic, or copy, the colors of the monarchs. This type of adaptation is called mimicry.

The bee orchid has markings on its petal that mimic a female bee. The flower gives off a scent that attracts male bees to the flower. This improves the flower's chances to reproduce.

© Houghton Mifflin Harcourt Publishing Company • Image Credits: (tl) ©Johanna Boomsma/Getty Images; (tr) ©U.S. Dept of Agriculture/Forest Service; (bl) ©Breck P. Kent/Animals Animals/Earth Scenes/National Geographic Stock; (br) ©David Clapp/Getty Images

Similar organisms live in very different environments. Mangrove trees and sand live oak trees look alike but have different adaptations. Mangrove trees grow in wet soil and typically get flooded two times each day. Most plants cannot survive in this much water. Sand live oak trees grow in dry soil and are able to survive long periods without water.

Mangrove tree

Sand live oak tree

Predict what would happen if a sand live oak tree was planted in the same environment as a mangrove tree. Explain your reasoning.

Vicuñas and camels are related. The camel on the left lives in the desert, while the vicuña on the right lives in the mountains. The vicuña's thick fur protects it in cold temperatures.

Camel

Vicuña

Basketball is often easier for taller people. Discuss with a classmate how to encourage someone who wants to play basketball but isn't tall.

© Houghton Mifflin Harcourt Publishing Company • Image Credits: (tl) ©Sune Wendelboe/Getty Images; (tr) ©Houghton Mifflin Harcourt; (bl) ©Christian Knospe/Fotolia; (br) ©Heath Korvola/Getty Images

The Same but Different

Just because two habitats have something in common does not mean that organisms there have the same adaptations. Compare the purple tansy and the bearberry that both live in dry environments.

Purple tansy grows in places that get little rain for long periods. Their seeds do not sprout until the rainy season, when the plant can get the moisture it needs.

Bearberry plants have thick, leathery leaves that keep moisture inside the plant during dry seasons with little rain.

Making Sense

How does understanding the relationship between an organism's adaptations and its habitat help you understand the octopus's behavior in its habitat?

© Houghton Mifflin Harcourt Publishing Company • Image Credits: (tr) ©Ernie Janes/Alamy; (bl) ©JeniFoto/Shutterstock

Lesson Check

Review your ideas from the beginning of this lesson about the octopus and its adaptations. How have your ideas changed? Be sure to do the following:

- Explain why the octopus changes color to blend in with its environment.
- Describe how changing color is both a physical and behavioral adaptation.
- Tell how camouflage is an adaptation.

Now I know or think that _____

_____

_____

Making Connections

Stone plants live in hot environments. They store water in their leaves. To avoid being eaten by animals, they have adapted to look like rocks. How are the stone plants similar to the octopus? How are they different?

_____

Checkpoints

1. Which best describes an example of camouflage?

    a. Blackberry bushes have thorns.

    b. Parrots have strong wings to fly.

    c. Viceroy butterflies look like monarch butterflies.

    d. Geckos change color to match their environment.

2. This cactus has spines. Spines are similar to thorns. How do spines help a cactus survive?

_____

_____

3. This parrot is well adapted for life in a tropical rain forest. Describe an environment that is not a good fit for the parrot. Identify a habitat where a parrot could not survive.

_____

_____

4. A vicuña lives on the ground in a cool mountain habitat. Which organism is least likely to survive in the same habitat as the vicuña?

a. goat

b. octopus

c. moose

d. wolf

5. Describe one physical or behavioral adaptation that helps a cat survive when outdoors.

_____

_____

_____

6. What environment do you think is best suited for a green frog? Give evidence to support your reasoning.

_____

_____

_____

Environments Change

Great day for a bike ride!

What do you notice about the bike path in the photo?

I notice _____

_____

_____

What do you wonder about how this bike path changed the environment?

I wonder _____

_____

_____

Can You Explain It?

How do you think a new bike path affects nearby organisms? Sketch, write, or model your answer.

Wild Horses

A **population** is made up of all the members of a certain kind of organism in an area. Populations must share resources, such as food and water.

Form a question Ask a question about how the availability of resources affects the size of a population.

© Houghton Mifflin Harcourt Publishing Company • Image Credits: ©Peter van Evert/ Alamy

Did you know?

A herd, or band, of horses is made of one male horse, female horses, and young.

STEP 1 Form two groups — one for horses and one for resources. Record the number of horses.

STEP 2 Each group member should make a card with their role on it. Resources should write either *food, water,* or *shelter* on their card.

STEP 3 The groups should line up facing each other. Each horse collects one resource. That resource joins the horses group. Record the number of horses.

STEP 4 Repeat Step 3 with each horse selecting a resource until they have all three resource types. Horses that cannot find a resource sit down.

Make a **claim** about how the size of a population affects available resources. Support your claim with **evidence** and explain your **reasoning**.

_____

_____

 Discuss with a neighbor how you handle sharing toys when there are more students than toys to play with.

Making Sense

How does understanding resource availability help you explain how building the bike path affects the availability of natural resources in the park?

_____

_____

Engineer It

How Can It Cross the Road?

Caribou live in forested areas. A city builds a highway through the forest, cutting the habitat in two parts. The caribou must find a way across the highway, which has changed the environment.

Form a question Ask a question about a way that humans can reduce the effects of changes they make to the environment.

Did you know?

Deforestation, or the cutting down of forests, disrupts the caribou's habitat.

Explore

STEP 1   **Explore**   What is the problem you need to solve?

_____

_____

What are two criteria for your solution?

_____

_____

_____

What is one constraint on your solution?

STEP 2   **Research**   Find out about caribou migration. What features of a solution would help the caribou safely cross the highway?

Make and Test

STEP 3   **Make**   Think of your own solution to the problem. Draw your idea below.

© Houghton Mifflin Harcourt Publishing Company • Image Credits: ©Houghton Mifflin Harcourt

STEP 4 **Share your solution** Group members should present their solutions. Discuss how each solution meets the criteria and constraints of the problem.

STEP 5 **Design a solution** Combine features of each idea to develop a team solution. Draw the team solution in the space below.

STEP 6 **Develop a model** Build a prototype, a model used for testing your solution.

STEP 7 **Make a plan** Write a plan to test your solution. Get your teacher's approval before you test your solution.

How does your team solution meet the criteria and constraint of the problem?

STEP 8 Share your solution with your class.

Improve and Test

STEP 9 Describe one improvement you could make to help more caribou safely cross the highway.

_____

_____

_____

Make a **claim** about the effect building a highway has on caribou migration. Support your claim with **evidence** from your investigation and explain your **reasoning**.

_____

_____

_____

_____

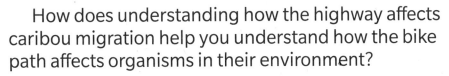

Making Sense

How does understanding how the highway affects caribou migration help you understand how the bike path affects organisms in their environment?

_____

_____

Everything Changes

Here Today, Different Tomorrow

Environments and organisms that interact with it form a system. Organisms are usually well adapted to survive in their environments. When an environment changes, the entire system is affected.

Wildfires spread quickly and drastically change an environment. The entire system changes.

Wildfires cause animals to lose their homes. Predict what a fox that lost its home in a fire would do next.

Different types of events change environments in many ways. Look at the photos below to learn more.

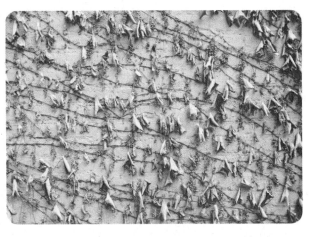

A volcano can cover land with lava and ash. Lava is melted rock from inside a volcano. It can change land. It may kill plants. The ash can cloud the sky so that the temperature of the land cools.

Drought, or lack of water, causes environments to dry out. This may cause plants to die. Animals may need to search for food and water elsewhere, or they also may die out.

Heavy rain may cause rivers, lakes, or streams to overflow.

When the land gives way in a mudslide, it takes trees and other plants with it.

Look at the photo of the flooding. How do you think this change affected the living things in the area?

Reacting to Change

Environmental changes affect living things by altering the landscape or changing the temperature of the area. Sometimes important resources are destroyed. After an environmental change, some organisms survive and are able to reproduce. Some animals are forced to leave and find new homes. Other animals move into the newly-changed environment. Unfortunately, many other organisms die.

During a wildfire, plants will die. But some plants still reproduce. Some pine trees have cones that release seeds after a fire. The seeds sprout on the ashy forest floor and grow into new plants.

The Amargosa vole only lives in certain parts of California. It depends on certain plants for food. During a drought, plants die, so voles move to new areas to find food.

This pika lives in the mountains of the Northwest. It must stay cool to survive. If an area becomes too warm, the pika must move farther north where the temperature is cooler.

 Think of a time that you faced a change in your life. How did you handle it? After you answer the question, turn to a classmate and discuss your answer with them. Write one experience below.

_____

_____

Making Sense

How does understanding the way that environmental changes affect organisms help you understand how the bike path affects the organisms in their environment?

_____

_____

Moving On Upstream

What Humans Can Do

You have seen a few ways that natural disasters can cause changes in the environment. Humans are another cause of environmental change that can impact living things. Read the captions with the images below to learn more about how humans can change the environment.

Humans clear land to make way for roads, highways, and walls. Animal and plant habitats are destroyed.

Dams change the habitats of animals that live around them. Dams also interfere with the habitats of fish and other animals that live in the water.

Humans do more to harm the environment than just building structures. Deforestation, or the cutting down of forests, disrupts plants and animals in many ways. It also negatively affects the climate and the human population. Humans may also introduce organisms into environments. These organisms that are not native to the area can compete with existing organisms for resources.

Humans may grow harmful plants by mistake. These plants are not native to an area. They take over the habitat of other plants, killing them and upsetting the balance of nature.

Humans cut down trees and clear land. This kills plants and destroys sources of food for animals that live there. Animals may move into areas where they would not normally be found.

Going Against the Flow

Salmon are born in freshwater rivers. Then, they swim downstream to the ocean. That is where they spend their adult lives. When they are fully grown, they swim upstream to the rivers to lay their eggs. However, humans have built dams between the ocean and the salmon's nesting places.

Salmon swimming upstream

A dam built by humans

What problem does a dam present for the salmon?

What two criteria should a solution to the problem meet?

What is a constraint that a solution to this problem must meet?

Engineers have used their understanding of scientific concepts along with research studies on salmon migration to design solutions to this problem. Read below to learn about some of these solutions.

This is a fish ladder. Salmon naturally leap out of the water. The salmon ladder uses this natural behavior to help salmon over the dam. When the salmon leap, they move up one step of the ladder. One step at a time, they get over the dam.

With a fish elevator, multiple fish swim into the elevator at the base of the dam. Once they get in, they can't get out until the elevator is raised and the fish swim out at the top of the dam.

A vertical-slot fish passage is another solution to the salmon problem. The fish swim through a slot at one side of the dam. The slot leads the fish up gentle ramps filled with water and pebbles. Eventually the fish find another slot to swim through. It's like swimming through a fish maze! At the end of the maze, the salmon are safely at the top of the dam.

Evaluate each of the solutions in the table below. Using your previous criteria and constraints, give each solution a rating from 1 to 5 (5 is best). In the constraint column, write *yes* or *no* if the solution meets the constraint.

Solution	Criteria #1 (1–5)	Criteria #2 (1–5)	Constraint (yes/no)

Based on your evaluation, which solution best solves the problem? Use evidence and reasoning to support your claim.

_____

_____

_____

●●●●

Making Sense

How does learning about human impacts on the environment help you understand the effects of changing the environment to build the bike path?

_____

_____

_____

Lesson Check

Can You Explain It?

Review your ideas from the beginning of this lesson about how the bike path affected the park. How have your ideas changed? Be sure to do the following:

- Identify the type of change the bike path was.
- Describe the effects the bike path had on organisms in the area.

Now I know that

Making Connections

This turtle is caught in litter that was left in its environment by humans. How is this human impact similar to that of the bike path? How is it different?

Checkpoints

1. Match each cause on the left to the effect it has on the environment.

building construction	survival and reproduction of some organisms
highway and dam construction	loss of habitat and food sources
wildfires	prevents animals from migrating

2. This is a photo of an oxbow lake. An oxbow lake forms when a river changes course and takes a straighter path, leaving a u-shaped loop off by itself. Describe how the formation of an oxbow lake may affect organisms living there.

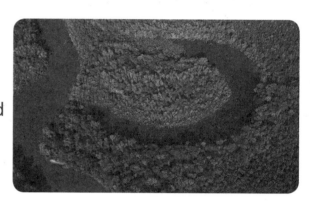

_____

_____

_____

3. What are some ways that an environment can change due to natural causes? Circle all that apply.

a. volcanic eruptions

b. beavers building dams

c. bridge construction and roads

d. dams that change the flow of water

4. Part of this organism's habitat is now an airport runway. Predict what you think will happen to the population. Provide evidence to support your reasoning.

5. To develop solutions to problems, engineers must use information from a variety of sources.

a. Explain how knowledge of science concepts help engineers come up with good solutions.

b. Explain why the results of research studies are an important source of knowledge for engineers.

6. Look at the data table below.

Year	Number of foxes
1	300
2	150
3	100

Describe what is likely happening to the available resources in this area. Cite evidence that supports your claim.

Evidence of Past Environments

What have we here?

What do you notice about the remains of this organism?

I notice _____

_____

_____

_____

What do you wonder about the remains of this organism?

I wonder _____

_____

_____

_____

Can You Explain It?

How do you think the remains of this fish ended up in a desert? Sketch, write, or model your answer.

How Do Fossils Form?

The remains of an organism that lived long ago are **fossils**. Fossils can form in different ways and tell you how long ago an organism lived.

Form a question   Ask a question that you can investigate about how fossils form.

© Houghton Mifflin Harcourt Publishing Company • Image Credits: ©Tom McHugh/ Science Source

> **Did you know?**
>
> The oldest known fossil is over 3.5 billion years old.

STEP 1 **Make a plan** Divide into four groups. Each group should choose a different type of fossil.

STEP 2 **Research** Find out more about your chosen fossil.

Describe how your fossil forms.

Explain how long it took your fossil to form.

STEP 3 **Develop a model** Use modeling clay to create your type of fossil from classroom objects. Draw your model below.

STEP 4 **Share information** Show your fossil to your class. Describe how your fossil formed and how old your fossil is.

STEP 5 **Develop an explanation** Describe other types of fossils and how they are made.

Make a **claim** about how the way a fossil forms allows scientists to estimate when it formed. Support your claim with **evidence** from your investigation and explain your **reasoning**.

Making Sense

How does understanding what fossils can tell us about the past help you explain why the fish fossil was in the desert?

What Can You Learn From a Fossil?

Fossils can tell you about different types of organisms and the environments in which they once lived. Some fossilized organisms no longer exist on Earth, and some environments have changed over time, too.

Form a question Ask a question that you can investigate about what fossils can tell us about past environments.

> **Did you know?**
>
> There are fossils of many kinds of organisms—even some bacteria!

_____

_____

STEP 1 **Investigate your question** Use the hand lens and your senses of sight and touch to observe the fossils your teacher gives you.

POSSIBLE MATERIALS

- ☐ fossil kit
- ☐ hand lens
- ☐ drawing paper
- ☐ crayons or colored pencils

STEP 2 **Collect data** Determine which of the fossils represent plants. Record the fossil number and your observations, such as leaf shape and size. Use a separate sheet of paper to make a table like the one below to record your observations. Share your results with others. Did you all classify your fossils in the same way?

Look!

Plant Fossils	
Fossil Number	**Observations**

STEP 3 Repeat the process for fossils that represent animals. Include the shape and size of limbs, body, teeth, and head, as well as other features.

STEP 4 **Develop an explanation** Select one of the fossils. Which fossil did you select? How did you know that this fossil was the remains of a plant or the remains of an animal?

_____

_____

_____

STEP 5 Research the environment in which this organism most likely lived. Draw and color a picture of the environment for your chosen fossil.

Which observations helped you decide what type of environment your fossilized organism lived in?

_____

_____

_____

Share your findings with others. What else did you learn about fossilized organisms?

What do you think scientists learn about organisms from the past when they study fossils?

 Were any of your ideas about the fossils incorrect? How might you help someone who was discouraged that his or her ideas were not correct?

Choose one of the animal fossils. Make a **claim** about the type of food it may have eaten based on your observation. Cite **evidence**, and explain your **reasoning**.

Making Sense

How does learning about fossils help you begin to understand the characteristics of the fish fossil?

© Houghton Mifflin Harcourt Publishing Company • Image Credits: ©Houghton Mifflin Harcourt

Evidence of Change

Fossils

Fossils can be made of an organism's hard parts or its soft parts. Hard parts include teeth, bones, and shells. Over time, these hard parts become rock. Often, an organism's soft parts—tissues such as skin and organs—are not preserved because they break down over time.

This shell was pressed into the soft mud on the sea floor. Over time, pressure changed the mud to rock. The shell dissolved and left a hollow space in the rock. Eventually mud filled the space to form an imprint of the shell.
....

Some soft-bodied organisms have been preserved by unique methods. Organisms can get trapped in sticky tree sap and die. As the sap hardens, the organisms become fossilized in the sap, or amber.
....

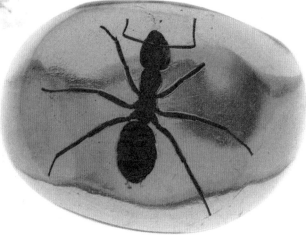

Turn to a partner and discuss other conditions that could preserve organisms. Write one condition below.

Fossils can form in various ways. Some fossils keep the organism just as it was when it died. Fossils can tell scientists about the behavior of animals that once roamed Earth. Look at the photos and read the captions below to learn more.

Some fossils tell us about the behavior of organisms that once lived. These footprints were made long ago in soft mud. Over time, the mud changed to rock and preserved the footprints. Footprints can tell scientists how large the organisms was, how quickly it moved, and if it traveled alone or in groups.

This petrified tree lived long ago. Petrified trees are often buried. Over millions of years, its wood is replaced by minerals. Normally, the outer shape of the wood is preserved, as well as its inner structure. Scientists can compare the inner structure of a petrified tree to modern day trees to identify the type of petrified tree.

Some organisms, such as this mammoth, can be preserved without becoming fossilized. This mammoth was trapped in ice for 40,000 years!

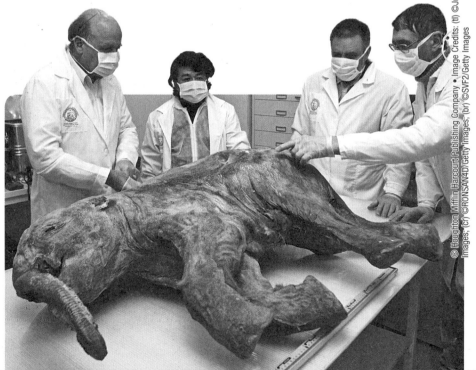

We Can Learn from the Past

Scientists will often study a present-day animal that is similar to a fossil. Patterns found in fossils and modern day animals can help scientists learn how the fossilized organism may have lived.

Ginkgo trees can reach heights of about 35 m and live up to 1,000 years.

Fossils show that ginkgo trees have not changed a lot in the last 100 million years.

The nautilus uses its tentacles to catch fish, crabs, and shrimp.

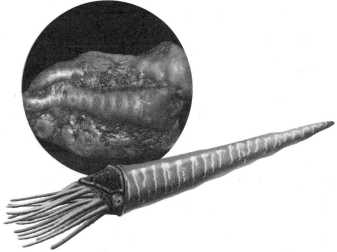

Fossils show similar ancient animals had long shells to protect their bodies.

 Turn to a classmate and explain to them how you might help someone that is frustrated because they are having trouble understanding this lesson.

A Closer Look

Fossils tell us much about the past. They can even tell us how some organisms changed over time. For example, woolly mammoths lived from about 10,000 to 5 million years ago, during the last ice age. Modern-day elephants, found in Africa and Asia, are related to woolly mammoths.

Compare List any features of the woolly mammoth that you think are similar to the elephant.

_____

_____

Contrast List any features of the woolly mammoth that you think differ from the elephant.

_____

_____

Why do you think elephants look different from woolly mammoths? Give evidence supporting your claim.

_____

_____

_____

Alive Today?

Some fossils look like organisms that live on Earth today. Others reveal **extinct** organisms—those no longer found on Earth. Fossils of extinct organisms provide clues as to how long life has been on Earth. We can also use fossils of extinct organisms to see how different organisms are related to one another.

This fossil is part of an ocean creature called a blastoid. It lived long ago and was anchored to the sea floor by a stemlike column. The picture shows what it might have looked like.

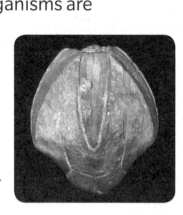

Fossil snail shells are evidence of an organism that once lived on Earth. At right is a modern snail on a leaf.

This fossil is a dinosaur's head. The picture shows what the animal might have looked like.

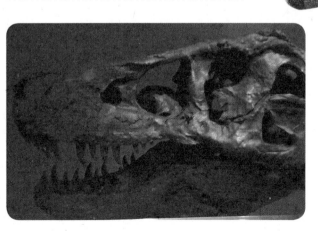

What Was That?

Some fossilized organisms are so strange that it can be hard to imagine what they looked like when they were alive! But, no matter how strange or common, fossils still provide scientists with evidence about life in the past.

Match the fossils on the left to the organisms on the right.

Making Sense

How does comparing fossils to organisms that are alive today help you begin to explain where the fossilized fish once lived?

_____

_____

Environments and Slow Change

Environments Change Over Time

Fossils tell us about the environments in which organisms lived. They can also tell us how environments have changed over time. As an environment changes, so do the plants and animals that live there.

Look at the fossils below. Write what it is on the lines below.

What evidence does each fossil provide for the type of organism that left it? In what kind of environment do you think each organism lived?

Ancient Aquatic Ecosystem

Think about the fossils you just looked at. They are the evidence of two prehistoric organisms, each from different environments. Look at the **aquatic,** or underwater, ecosystem below. It existed about 400 million years ago. This environment no longer looks exactly like this.

Identify each organism based on its description.

a. The head of this fish was covered with armored plates, and the rest of its body was covered with thick scales.

b. These looked like present-day clams. Thick shells protected their soft bodies. Remains of their shells can be found as fossils today.

c. Feather stars are related to modern-day sea stars. They lived attached to the sea floor.

d. These organisms lived inside a long shell. They were related to present-day squids and octopuses.

Choose an organism above and identify an adaptation that made it well-suited to its environment.

© Houghton Mifflin Harcourt Publishing Company

Ancient Terrestrial Ecosystem

Take a look at this **terrestrial,** or land, ecosystem from 50,000 to 11,000 years ago. Read about these organisms and how they may have interacted with each other. This environment, and the organisms that inhabit it, have changed over time.

Identify each organism based on its description below.

a. This ancient bird was over 1 m tall. Its wings were about 3 m long. It also had long legs, neck, and bill.

b. A saber-toothed cat had long, sharp front teeth, called sabers, which could be 30 cm in length.

c. Plants from thousands of years ago may have looked different from modern plants. But they still functioned in much the same way.

d. The dire wolf was about the same length as a modern-day gray wolf, but it weighed more.

Choose an organism and identify an adaptation that made it well-suited to its environment.

The photos below show fossils of the organisms you observed in the illustrations on the previous pages. These fossils were used to identify features of each organism, which helped scientists determine their environments.

Dire wolf

Ancient fish

Oak leaves

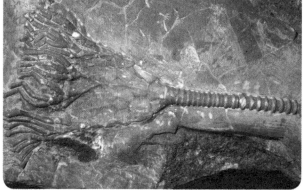

Feather star

Compare these organisms from aquatic and terrestrial ecosystems. What characteristics helped the organisms survive in their environments?

Common Features

What do scientists do when there are no animals alive today that are very similar to an extinct fossil organism? They look for living animals that have some features similar to the fossil. This can help scientists learn about the type of environment in which the extinct organism lived.

Complete the chart to identify an organism living today that is similar in structure to the fossils below. What physical features does your animal have in common with the fossil?

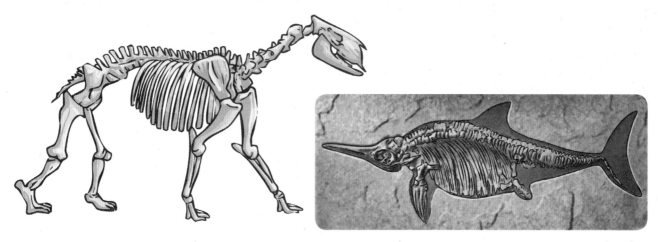

Fossil A　　　　　　　　　　　　**Fossil B**

	Similar organism	Similar features
Fossil A		
Fossil B		

In what type of environment do you think each fossil organism lived?

You Found It Where?

Scientists have found fossils of organisms that lived in oceans in areas of dry land today. How could a fossil of an organism that lived in one environment be found in an environment that is totally different today?

The plant in the image above lived from about 300 to 200 million years ago. It dropped its leaves in the cooler season, and grew new leaves during warmer seasons. The plant grew all over the large landmass that existed during that time period. Today, the area is a snowy mountain range.

Describe the environment in which this plant lived.

_____

_____

Making Sense

How does learning about the differences between current and past environments help you explain why the fish fossil was found in a desert?

_____

_____

© Houghton Mifflin Harcourt Publishing Company • Image Credits: (t) ©Gordon Wiltsie/Getty Images; (inset) ©Nature/UIG/Getty Images

Lesson Check

Can You Explain It?

Review your ideas from the beginning of this lesson about the fish fossil in a desert. How have your ideas changed?

Be sure to do the following:

- Compare the animal with similar organisms living today.
- Include evidence about the fish's environment.
- Explain what finding the fish fossil in a desert tells us.

Now I know that _____

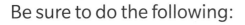

_____

Making Connections

This fossil of a terrestrial animal was found in a modern-day aquatic environment. How is this similar to the fossil at the beginning of the lesson? How is it different?

_____

_____

Checkpoints

1. Write the name of each feature under the environment in which it would be found. Give an example of a modern-day organism that has this feature.

tentacles	fins	leaves
wings	flippers	feet

Terrestrial	Aquatic

2. Observe the fossil in the photo. Think about what this fossilized organism once looked like. Sketch an image of the organism in the space below.

3. What can scientists learn from studying fossils? Circle all that apply.

  a. conditions of past environments

  b. how organisms moved, what they ate, and how they interacted

  c. how fossil organisms may be related to organisms alive today

  d. what sounds different animals made in the past

4. A strong storm knocked this tree over. The wood is starting to rot. Explain below whether or not this is a fossil.

5. Several fossils were recently discovered in a desert environment. Use the data below to answer the question.

Unknown Fossilized Organisms	
Fossil Number	**Observations**
1	organism has long neck, four legs, and a long tail
2	organism has two fins, a short tail, and a long mouth
3	organism has two flippers, a wide tail, and a fin

Describe the environment in which Organism 3 likely lived. Describe the environment in which the fossil was found. Explain how this is possible.

6. Which is the most likely reason that modern-day elephants have less fur than woolly mammoths? Circle the best answer.

a. The mammoths lived on land, while elephants live in the water.

b. The mammoths lived in the water, and elephants live on land.

c. The mammoths lived in a much warmer climate.

d. The mammoths lived in a much colder climate.

Unit Review

1. Observe the Arctic poppies below.

Morning

Evening

Arctic poppies change throughout the day. Write a cause-and-effect statement about how the environment affects the arctic poppies.

_____

_____

_____

2. Select all the ways that adaptations can help an organisms in its environment.

a. reproduce   **c.** use less energy when food is scarce

b. hunt prey   **d.** protection from predators

3. Identify two turtle adaptations. Use these as evidence to support an argument that they help it survive in its environment.

_____

_____

© Houghton Mifflin Harcourt Publishing Company

4. Match the cause on the left to the effect it has on the environment.

| highway | reduced survival and reproduction of some organisms |

| clearing land to make room for a new mall | prevents animals from migrating |

| tornadoes | loss of habitat and food sources |

5. Can people be affected by their environment? Make an argument using evidence to support your claim.

_____

_____

6. Observe the system in the photo. Describe the features that make it suitable for this deer. Then, give an example of an organism that would not survive here. Use evidence to support your argument.

_____

_____

_____

7. While hiking, you find the bones of an animal that died recently. Did you find a fossil? Explain your reasoning.

_____

8. This fossil of a turtle was found on an island where temperatures today are about –20 °C (–4 °F). Sketch what you think the environment was like when the turtle was alive.

9. Write a cause-and-effect statement that describes how an earthquake changed this environment. Describe two results of the change.

10. A community wants a bridge built so that animals can safely cross a highway. The bridge must allow different types of animals to cross it, not change the environment very much, and be cheap. A company proposes to build a large and heavy steel bridge.

Consider the merits of the proposed solution. Use evidence to argue for or against it.

In Unit 4, you constructed explanations about the patterns in how organisms survived when the environment changed. In this unit, you will collect and analyze data to explain patterns in weather can vary by season or by regions in the world.

UNIT 5 Weather Impacts

We Can Predict Weather

I'm falling for this weather!

What do you notice about the weather in the image?

I notice _____

_____

_____

_____

What do you wonder about how the weather might change?

I wonder _____

_____

_____

_____

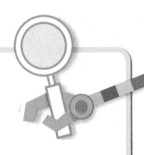

Can You Explain It?

How can the trees and sky in this image help you predict what the weather will be like in the next few months? Sketch, write, or model your answer.

Weather Here and There

This is the capital building in Jefferson City, Missouri. The weather in the photo is sunny, but that doesn't mean it is sunny everywhere. You'll take a closer look at the weather in different locations in this activity.

Form a question Ask a question about weather patterns in different locations.

Did you know?

Late June through late September are winter in the Southern Hemisphere!

MATERIALS

☐ map of the United States (3 per group)

☐ newspaper or Internet

STEP 1 **Make a plan** Look at your map and locate three cities that you think experience different types of weather. List the three cities,and explain why you chose them.

_____

_____

STEP 2 **Research** With your partner, research the average high temperatures in your cities for the months of April, May, and June.

_____

_____

STEP 3 **Organize your data** Use a separate sheet of paper to make a data table. Record your data.

Look at your data. Which city had the highest average temperature each month?

Hmm.

April: _____

May: _____

June: _____

Analyze your data Use your data table to draw a bar graph for the month of June for each city.

Use the bar graph to make a **claim** about which city would have the highest average temperature in July. Support your claim with **evidence** from your investigation, and explain your **reasoning**.

Making Sense

How does exploring how temperatures change over time help you begin to explain how the weather in the image might be different in a few months?

Regional Weather

Weather data is collected from all around the world every day. Meteorologists are people who study weather data. They look for patterns in the data so they can make predictions about the weather.

Form a question Ask a question about how learning about weather helps meteorologists.

Did you know?

Large cities with temperatures higher than surrounding areas are known as urban heat islands.

STEP 1 **Make a plan** Look at the key on your map. Use the key to select the correct colored pencils to use with this activity.

Which color will you use to show each temperature below on the map?

85 °F: _____

68 °F: _____

50 °F: _____

MATERIALS

☐ data from previous investigation

☐ state capital maps (3 per group) and 1 class map

☐ colored pencils

STEP 2 **Develop a model** Use your data from the last investigation and the map key. Fill in the circle for each city you researched on the map for the month of April.

STEP 3 Repeat step 2 for both the May and June maps.

 Sometimes people have difficulties with tasks or answering questions. How could you support someone who is having a difficult time completing this activity?

_____

_____

_____

STEP 4 **Organize data** When you have finished filling in your maps, wait for your turn, and then go to the classroom map. Use the correct colors to transfer your data to the class map.

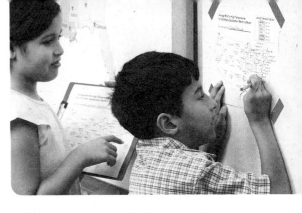

STEP 5 **Analyze data** Look at the classroom maps for each month. What patterns in the colors on the map do you see over those three months?

Draw conclusions Make a **claim** about what you would see on the map for the month of July. Use **evidence** from your investigation, and explain your **reasoning**.

Making Sense

How does seeing the change in temperatures over a larger area help you understand how you can predict weather in the area with the colorful trees?

A Year of Change

Give It a Year

If the weather changes over three months, think about how it might change over a year. These images show how the weather in Chicago changes during a year. Observe how the weather changes from month to month and season to season.

January is winter. The weather is cold, and snowstorms are common. People wear warm clothes this time of year.

March is spring. The weather gets warmer, and strong winds can blow. Snow can often still be seen this time of year.

Thunderstorms roll through the city on hot summer afternoons in July. Summer months in Chicago can be quite hot.

Fall starts in September. Some days are cloudy and gray. Temperatures are cooler. This is the time of year when leaves on trees begin to change colors.

Circle all of the statements that describe the weather throughout the year in Chicago.

a. March can be windy.

b. Snowstorms are common in September.

c. January can be stormy with lots of snow.

d. Hot weather in July can bring afternoon thunderstorms.

The direction from which wind travels is one weather condition that changes over time. This table shows the average wind direction in Chicago each month.

Month	Wind direction
January	west
February	west
March	west
April	south
May	southwest
June	southwest
July	southwest
August	southwest
September	south
October	south
November	southwest
December	west

a. Look at the data in the data table. Describe any patterns you see.

_____

_____

_____

_____

b. In which seasons do the patterns you observed occur?

_____

_____

_____

Seasonal Changes

Look at the table with a classmate. Use the average seasonal temperatures in the data table to answer the questions below.

	Spring	Summer	Autumn	Winter
Year 1	44 °F	71 °F	51 °F	22 °F
Year 2	49 °F	71 °F	55 °F	28 °F
Year 3	51 °F	69 °F	55 °F	29 °F
Year 4	47 °F	72 °F	50 °F	19 °F

Suppose you were going to make a prediction for Year 5 based on the patterns in the data. Make a **claim** about which season would be the easiest to predict. Support your claim with **evidence** from the table, and explain your **reasoning**.

Which season is most likely to average 46 °F in Year 5? Explain your reasoning.

Turn to someone next to you, and share one part of this lesson that you found difficult.

© Houghton Mifflin Harcourt Publishing Company

Weather conditions such as temperature and precipitation are always changing. Meteorologists measure these conditions every day. They find the average of the measurements. Average measurements help meteorologists see patterns in the weather. The data help them understand how the weather changes over time.

Pick one year from the table and draw a bar graph showing each season.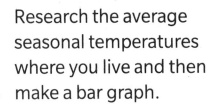

Research the average seasonal temperatures where you live and then make a bar graph.

Making Sense

How does understanding seasonal changes help you predict what the weather in the image of the colorful trees might be like in the future?

Predicting Weather

Finding Patterns

Some cities may get a lot of rain in the fall. Other cities might get most of their precipitation in the spring. You can use these patterns to make weather predictions.

Look at the table. Some data are missing. Use the patterns you observe to fill in the missing data using temperatures shown.

Anchorage, AK

79 °F   63 °F   56 °F   80 °F   60 °F   30 °F   44 °F   14 °F

	Monthly Average Temperature (°F)			
	Riverside, CA		Anchorage, AK	
	Year 1	Year 2	Year 1	Year 2
January	53	53	13	14
February	55		17	
March	60	60	30	22
April	63		33	35
May	65	69		46

Describe the pattern you see in the data and how this pattern helps you fill in the missing data.

_____

_____

_____

The table below shows monthly precipitation totals for two cities across two years. Look for patterns in the data. Then, use your observations to answer the questions below.

Total Monthly Precipitation (inches)				
	Fargo, ND		Portland, ME	
	Year 1	Year 2	Year 1	Year 2
January	1	0	3	2
February	1	1	8	3
March	1	5	6	3
April	2	1	4	5
May	2	2	1	5

Portland, ME

Which city receives more precipitation for these months?

_____

_____

Does temperature or precipitation show a more predictable pattern? Explain your reasoning.

_____

_____

_____

Why is it important for scientists to collect weather data?

_____

_____

_____

Weather Patterns

Look at the bar graph below. It shows precipitation in Honolulu, Hawaii, in the Pacific Ocean. Use the data in the bar graph to make a pictograph in the space below.

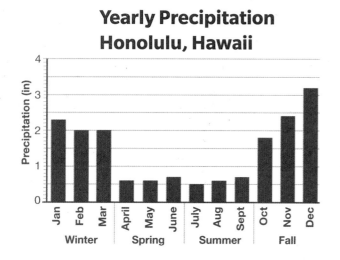

Use the bar graph or pictograph to predict which month will have the most precipitation next year. Explain your answer.

Making Sense

How does analyzing past weather data help you predict how the weather can change in the location in the image of colorful trees?

Lesson Check

Can You Explain It?

Review your ideas from the beginning of this lesson about predicting the weather. How have your ideas changed? Be sure to do the following:

- Identify the season in the image.
- Explain how seasonal patterns help you make predictions.
- Predict what the weather will be like in a few months.

Now I know that _____

_____

_____

_____

Making Connections

This image shows the weather in a different location. How is it similar to the location at the beginning of the lesson? How is it different?

_____

_____

_____

© Houghton Mifflin Harcourt Publishing Company • Image Credits: (t) ©Denis Jr. Tangney/iStock/Getty Images Plus/Getty Images; (b) ©Martin Battilana Photography/ Alamy

Checkpoints

Look at the data tables. Use the data to answer the questions below.

1. Predict which months are most likely to have snow next year in Denver. It must be 32 °F or below for snow to occur.

   a. February

   b. December

   c. April

   d. September

   e. January

2. Predict which three months in Denver will have the hottest temperatures next year.

   _____

   _____

   _____

3. Predict which three months will have the least precipitation next year in Miami.

   a. September, October, November

   b. March, April, May

   c. June, July, August

   d. December, January, February

Denver, Colorado

Month	Average temperature
January	31 °F
February	32 °F
March	48 °F
April	50 °F
May	57 °F
June	67 °F
July	74 °F
August	72 °F
September	62 °F
October	50 °F
November	39 °F
December	30 °F

Miami, Florida

Month	Total precipitation
January	2 inches
February	2 inches
March	3 inches
April	3 inches
May	5 inches
June	10 inches
July	7 inches
August	9 inches
September	10 inches
October	6 inches
November	3 inches
December	2 inches

4. You look at the data for average Chicago temperatures each month. You see average temperatures of 47 °F, 59 °F, and 70 °F. Which three months are you most likely looking at?

a. March, April, May

c. August, September, October

b. July, August, September

d. September, October, November

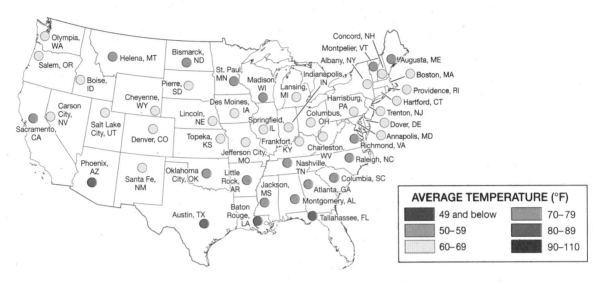

5. The map above shows the average temperature for the month of April. Make a claim that predicts how the map will look in the month of May. Use evidence and reasoning to support your claim.

6. Which statistic shows a pattern in weather data? Circle the best answer.

a. total precipitation of 4 in. in June

b. average temperature of 50 °F in June, 65 °F in July, and 60 °F in August

c. average temperature of 60 °F in July and 39 °F in November

d. record-high precipitation of 10 in. in August

It's very breezy here!

What do you notice about this machine?

I notice _____

_____

_____

What do you wonder about the purpose of this machine?

I wonder _____

_____

_____

Can You Explain It?

How is this machine used to make people safer? Sketch, write, or model your answer.

The Answer Is Blowing in the Wind

There are patterns of wind all around the world. Sometimes, wind can be very dangerous. In the image above, the wind is useful because it helps dry the laundry.

Form a question Ask a question about the effect of wind strength on objects.

Did you know?

The fastest non-tornado wind ever recorded was a 253-mph gust!

STEP 1 **Investigate your question**
Open your textbook to its
middle. Place your mouth even
with the top page and blow
gently on the page. Then, blow
with more strength.

STEP 2 **Organize data** Record the
results of your trials below.

STEP 3 Close your book, and repeat Step 1.

Draw conclusions Make a **claim** about how the strength
of the wind is related to the amount of change it can cause.
Support your claim with **evidence** from your investigation,
and explain your **reasoning**.

Making Sense

How did this investigation help you understand the
purpose of the wind machine?

Engineer It
Smashing Weather

Many types of weather can be dangerous. Snowy and icy roads can cause accidents. People try to find ways to stay safe in snowy or icy conditions and during other dangerous weather events.

Form a question Ask a question that you can investigate about protecting people and property from severe weather.

> **Did you know?**
>
> The most snowfall recorded in a 24-hour period was 75 2/3 inches!

POSSIBLE MATERIALS

- ☐ goggles
- ☐ pan
- ☐ sand
- ☐ water
- ☐ water containers
- ☐ model house
- ☐ small stones
- ☐ plastic straws
- ☐ strips of fabric

Explore

STEP 1   **Research**   Look up a type of severe weather and the problems it can cause.

STEP 2   **Define the problem**   What problem related to severe weather are you trying to solve?

What is one constraint and one criteria for your solution?

STEP 3   **Develop a model**   Develop multiple solutions. Then, draw a model of your chosen solution.

Make and Test

STEP 4   Write how you will test your model. Get your teacher's approval. Then, run a test.

How well did your solution meet the criteria and constraints of the problem?

Improve and Test

STEP 5   How can you improve your solution? Sketch your new design below.

STEP 6   **Draw conclusions** Build and test your new model. How did your new model perform?

STEP 7 **Share information** Compare your solution to other groups' solutions and their results. What did you find?

Turn to a neighbor and discuss ways to comment on someone's solution in a respectful way.

Make a **claim** about how testing models helps make solutions better. Support your claim with **evidence** from your investigation, and explain your **reasoning.**

Aha!

Making Sense

How does this investigation help you understand the purpose of the machine from the beginning of this lesson?

Cause-and-Effect Weather

Severe Weather Threats

Some effects of weather are hard to see. Other effects of weather are observed every day. And even more effects are quite easy to see. Severe weather is any type of weather that can harm people or property.

Describe severe weather you have observed.

A tornado is a swirling column of fast-moving air. Tornadoes form when cold and warm air meet. This can cause the air to rotate. Tornaodoes damage property and hurt people. Some tornadoes are stronger, faster, and more violent than others. They are most common in the spring and fall.

Hurricanes are huge storms with heavy rain and winds of 74 mph or more. They form over oceans. When they move over land, the winds and rising waters can cause flooding and major damage. Hurricanes are most common in the summer and fall.

Lightning is a big danger during thunderstorms. Some lightning strikes cause injuries and even deaths. Lightning often hits objects and causes fires. A direct hit from lightning can split trees.

A blizzard is a winter snowstorm with strong winds and blowing snow. Winds in a blizzard reach 35 mph or more. Blowing snow can make it hard to see. Ice can make roads slippery. Many car and truck accidents happen from icy roads and blowing snow.

Weather Makes It Happen

Severe weather can bring all kinds of risks. Different areas have different types of severe weather. Most tornadoes occur in the United States. In fact, the central part of the United States is called Tornado Alley. In the United States, hurricanes threaten the Gulf and East coasts in summer and early fall. Hurricanes can damage large areas. People who live where severe weather occurs need to be prepared.

Look at the images of damage that severe weather can cause. On the lines below, write the type of weather that may have caused the damage. Some types of damage can be caused by more than one type of weather.

 How could you help someone that might have had to move due to damage from severe weather?

Name That Weather

Because it is in the middle of the United States, St. Louis has had many tornadoes. The worst one was in 1896. In January of 1982, St. Louis suffered through a blizzard that dropped 13 inches of snow. Drifts piled as high as 7 feet. On average, St. Louis has thunderstorms 48 days every year.

It's hot for a fall day in St. Louis—80 °F and sunny. In the late afternoon, the white puffy clouds grow taller and darker. The sun disappears, and gusty winds start to blow. Heavy rain falls, and thunder follows flashes of lightning. Within an hour, the rain has stopped and the sun is shining again.

What possible weather hazards might the storm in St. Louis have caused?

Making Sense

How does understanding severe weather help you understand why engineers use wind machines for testing?

Reducing Risk

How Scientists Do It

Scientists who study the weather are called *meteorologists*. They collect data about weather that has already happened. This helps them predict weather events in the future.

Meteorologists want to predict severe weather accurately. Most severe weather also brings weather hazards. A **hazard** is something that can cause damage to a person or property.

Weather radar and satellites help meteorologists observe weather that is currently happening. They can also see which direction that weather is headed. This helps them predict where severe weather is going to happen.

Engineering for Weather

We can't stop severe weather. But people have designed solutions that protect people and property from hazards related to weather. People can find different ways to reduce weather hazards. Engineers work to design structures to decrease the amount of damage caused by severe weather. For example, to stop water from coming into a building in a hurricane, walls on the first level can be made of brick or stone that will hold up to floodwaters.

When the conditions are just right, precipitation falls as ice instead of rain or snow. Heavy ice coats trees, power lines, streets, sidewalks, and bridges.

Foggy conditions are very hazardous, especially for people who are driving.

Severe Weather Solutions

Engineers solve severe weather issues in a variety of ways. Sometimes engineers improve an existing technology to make it better. Other times engineers develop new technologies to solve a problem. These solutions help protect people and property from the hazards of severe weather. Each has benefits and drawbacks.

A lightning rod is a metal rod attached to a tall building or structure. It is designed to attract lightning during a thunderstorm. It directs the energy safely into the ground.

A snow plow removes large amounts of snow from streets. But it dumps the snow in large piles that can block sidewalks or trap parked cars on the sides of roads.

Solar roadways and sidewalks are both examples of solutions currently being tested. They are designed with solar panels that you can drive, walk, and park on. Engineers hope that the panels will be able to store enough energy from the sun to melt ice and snow. They are testing to be sure that the roads can stand up to heavy traffic and that all of the features of the roadway work correctly.

What is the cause-effect-relationship between severe weather and the solutions designed to help deal with it?

What is a severe weather solution where you live?

Select the Best

Complete the table below to identify the pros and cons of the severe weather solutions you read about.

Pros			
Cons			

Which solution do you think is best at protecting people from the hazards of severe storms? Explain your choice. Discuss the good and bad points of the solution and its design with a classmate. Discuss until you both agree.

●●●●

Making Sense

How does evaluating severe weather solutions help you understand the importance of using the wind machine for testing?

Lesson Check

Can You Explain It?

Review your ideas from the beginning of the lesson about the function of the wind machine. How have your ideas changed?

Be sure to do the following:

- Identify the type of weather being modeled.
- Tell how these tests help keep people safe from severe weather.

Now I know that _____

_____

_____

Making Connections

This structure uses Doppler radar. It helps track severe weather. How is this like the wind machine at the beginning of the lesson? How is it different?

_____

_____

_____

Checkpoints

1. Choose the correct word from the word bank to complete the sentences.

criteria	predictions	severe	property
data	good	nice	designs

We can record patterns of weather to make

_____ about what kind of weather might

happen next. Meteorologists issue warnings about

_____ weather to help people protect

themselves and their _____ from harm.

2. Circle all the effects that could be caused by a tornado.

   a. rivers overflowing their banks

   b. roads washed away by flooding

   c. trees torn out of the ground

   d. buildings with crumbled walls

3. Which of these solutions could reduce the impact of weather hazards? Circle all that apply.

   a. sandbags piled up along a flooding river

   b. foghorns during dense fog

   c. cutting grass before a thunderstorm

   d. lightning rods during a thunderstorm

4. Your friend designs a jacket for staying dry when it rains. It is made out of yellow cloth and has a collar but no hood. Which changes to the design would make it keep someone more dry when it rains? Circle all that apply.

a. Add a hood to keep your head dry.

b. Add stripes that reflect light so people can see you.

c. Make the jacket out of black cloth.

d. Add a way to make the cuffs on the wrist fit tighter.

e. Make the jacket out of waterproof material.

5. It's the first day of winter. Predict a type of severe weather that may occur within the next six weeks. What weather pattern is evidence for your argument?

6. Label each solution with the severe weather from which it protects.

Types of Climates

Are these guys on vacation??

What do you notice about the blue penguins?

I notice _____

_____

_____

What do you wonder about the weather where these blue penguins live?

I wonder _____

_____

_____

Can You Explain It?

How are the weather patterns where these blue penguins live different from other locations? Sketch, write, or model your answer.

Feel the Heat!

This island is often hot and gets a lot of rain. Other islands are cold and get a lot of snow. There are many different weather patterns on Earth.

Form a question Ask a question about different types of weather on Earth.

© Houghton Mifflin Harcourt Publishing Company • Image Credits: ©Lucky-photographer/Alamy

Did you know?

The hottest recorded temperature on Earth is 134 °F!

STEP 1 Blow up the globe if it is not already blown up.

STEP 2 **Investigate your question**
Touch the North Pole, equator, and South Pole. Describe how they feel.

MATERIALS

☐ globe, clear plastic

☐ hair dryer (teacher only)

STEP 3 **Collect data** Your teacher will use a hair dryer to direct hot air toward the equator on your model for one minute. Do not put the ball too close to the hair dryer. Predict how the temperature will change at each location. Then, check each location. How does each location feel?

Draw conclusions Make a **claim** about what the hair dryer represents in your model. Cite **evidence**, and explain your **reasoning.**

Making Sense

How does this investigation help you begin to understand the differences in the weather patterns where the penguins live?

Looking for a New Home

This rain forest is very different from where the blue penguins live in Australia. Suppose the penguins have to be moved to a new location. How could you determine where to move them? What kind of location would work?

Form a question Ask a question about weather differences around the world.

Did you know?

The Amazon in South America is the largest rain forest in the world.

STEP 1 **Make a plan** Choose a location on the map that you think might be suitable for the blue penguin. Which location will you research, and why?

STEP 2 **Research** Find out the weather patterns in your location and those in Adelaide, Australia, where blue penguins live. Find monthly data for temperature and precipitation for one year. On a separate sheet of paper, record the data from both locations in a table.

Think about how you can work together as a team to research and record your data. Share your ideas with your group.

How will these data help you determine whether the location you chose is good for the penguins?

STEP 3 Write the location and weather pattern data on a self-stick note. Place the note on the map near your location.

STEP 4 Compare your data for all locations on the map to data for Adelaide. Which location has the most similar temperature pattern? Which location has the most similar rain pattern?

STEP 5 Discuss your comparisons with another group. Decide which locations would not work as a habitat for the blue penguins. Eliminate those locations. Which locations did you eliminate? Why?

STEP 6 Choose any location with weather patterns similar to Adelaide. With your group, research five more years of data to determine if the weather patterns in the place you chose are consistent. Which location did you choose? Would the weather patterns support a blue penguin colony?

STEP 7 **Draw conclusions** Look at the locations on the map and compare their distances from the equator. Do you see any pattern in the weather and each city's distance from the equator? If so, what is it?

Are any of the locations on the map similar in distance from the equator to Adelaide? If so, which one?

Make a **claim** about how analyzing patterns in weather data helped you find a good location to relocate the blue penguins. Cite **evidence**, and explain your **reasoning**.

Making Sense

How did this investigation help you begin to understand the differences in weather patterns where the blue penguin lives compared to other locations?

Out of Place

Different Birds, Different Homes

Different penguins live in different places around the world. The map shows where two species of penguin live. How do the emperor penguin and the blue penguin look the same? How do they look different? Now, compare their habitats. How are the places where they live the same and different?

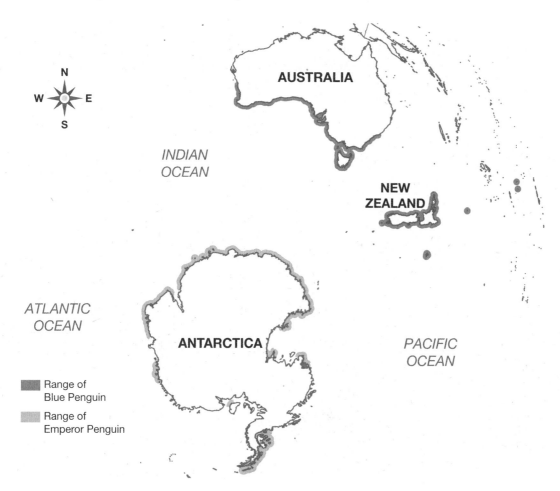

Even though the penguins live in different habitats, they share a pattern in where they live. Use the maps to identify the pattern.

Emperor penguins are the largest penguin species, standing about 1 m (40 in.) tall. Emperors live on the frozen coast of Antarctica. They fish for food in icy waters. Emperor penguins live on the open ice during the harsh winter. They huddle in large groups to keep warm. Antarctica also has cold summers.

The blue penguin is the smallest penguin species. They are also called fairy penguins or little penguins. Blue penguins stand only about 33 cm (13 in.) tall. The emperor penguin is about three times taller than the blue penguin. The blue penguins live on the southern coast of Australia and on the coast of New Zealand. They make nests in burrows on coastal sand dunes or in openings between rocks on the shore. Like other penguins, blue penguins eat fish that they catch in coastal waters.

 You spend a lot of time at school. Turn to a classmate and tell them what parts of school make you feel most comfortable.

Feels Like Home

Climate is the normal weather in an area over a long period of time. When you say that it is warm outside today, you are describing the weather. When you say that the weather is warm in summer, you are describing climate.

View the photos. They show various locations in New Zealand throughout the year. As you look at the photos, think about the climate where the blue penguin lives.

The penguins live in a part of New Zealand with a mild climate. The normal high winter temperature is about 53 °F. Winter is the wettest season.

Normal daytime spring temperatures in northern New Zealand are about 60 °F. Coastal wildflowers in the penguin's nesting area start to bloom in springtime.

Days become cooler in fall on the northern coast of New Zealand. But temperatures stay mild, and clouds bring many days of rain.

The penguins on the northern coast of New Zealand live in a climate where summers are warm and have a lot of rain.

How would you describe the climate in New Zealand?

Climate Is Everywhere

Observe Earth's climate zones. Each climate zone has certain general features. However, areas within each zone can have different features than what is normal. Use the correct letter from each description below to label the map on the next page.

A Tropical Zones

These climate zones are the hottest. It is hot or warm all year. Places near the equator have heavy rain throughout the year. Places farther from the equator have wet and dry seasons.

B Temperate Zones

These climate zones have hot or warm summers and cool or cold winters. Precipitation falls as both rain and snow in some places in these zones. Other parts are dry.

C Polar Zones

These climate zones are the coldest. They have cold winters and cool summers. Precipitation is usually light, and most of it is snow.

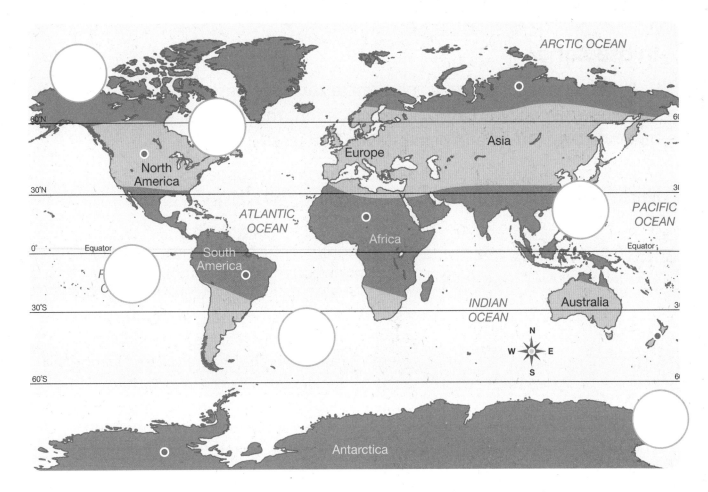

Circle the temperature and precipitation description that describes each climate zone. Go back and look at the map and climate zone descriptions, if needed.

Climate zone	Temperature	Precipitation
Polar	• cold or cool all year • cold only in winter	• light rain in the winter • mostly snow
Temperate	• hot summers, warm winters • hot or warm summers, cool or cold winters	• wet summers, dry winters • wet and dry areas; winter snowfall
Tropical	• hot or warm all year • hot summers, cold winters	• light or no precipitation • heavy rain all year at the equator

© Houghton Mifflin Harcourt Publishing Company

In the Zone

How can you figure out which climate zone a place is in? If you have a map, you can look at its location. You can also observe temperature and precipitation patterns.

Look at the temperature and precipitation data for each city below. Then, identify the climate zone for each city.

a. Nairobi is a city in Kenya, a country in eastern Africa. Nairobi is in the mountains, which makes the weather a little different from that in surrounding areas. Cities that are in the mountains are cooler than nearby cities. Nairobi gets most of its rain in the spring.
- high temperature: 83 °F in summer
- low temperature: 53 °F in winter
- highest amount of precipitation: about 6 in. in November
- lowest amount of precipitation: about ½ in. in July

Climate zone: _____

b. Upernavik is a town in Greenland. It is on the coast of Baffin Bay. People might need coats in the middle of summer in Upernavik, but they rarely need umbrellas.
- high temperature: 46 °F in summer
- low temperature: −10 °F in winter
- highest amount of precipitation: about 1 in. in July
- lowest amount of precipitation: about ⅓ in. in March

Climate zone: _____

Not Always the Same

Most of the time, the climate for a location stays similar from year to year. Sometimes, the weather does not follow normal patterns during the year. Look at the images below and on the next page. They show three ways this can happen.

An El Niño occurs when waters in the Pacific Ocean are warmer than normal. As a result, climate patterns change.

During the 1982–1983 El Niño, heavy rains caused severe flooding in Peru. Australia had a harmful drought.

During a La Niña, waters in the Pacific Ocean are cooler than normal. La Niña also affects global climate patterns.

During a La Niña in 2010–2011, the southern part of the United States had less rain than normal.

Mount Pinatubo is a volcano that erupted in 1991. It sent a huge cloud of ash and harmful gas 35 km (22 mi) into the air.

The cloud of ash circled Earth. It blocked the sun's energy, causing temperatures to be lower than normal around the world for about two years.

Making Sense

How does learning about the different climate zones help you understand the differences between where the blue penguin lives and other areas on Earth?

Lesson Check

Can You Explain It?

Review your ideas about climate from the beginning of this lesson. How have your ideas changed? Be sure to:

- explain why you couldn't move the blue penguin to just any location on Earth.
- describe features of the different climate zones.

Now I know that _____

_____

_____

Making Connections

This polar bear lives in the Arctic. How is the Arctic climate similar to where the blue penguin lives? How is it different?

_____

_____

_____

Checkpoints

1. In the spring, the weather is cool, and there is some rain. By summer, the temperatures are much higher, and there is little rain. When fall comes, the temperatures cool off, and there is some rain. In winter, it is very cold, and there is usually some snow on the ground. Which climate zone does this describe?

   a. forest zone

   b. tropical zone

   c. polar zone

   d. temperate zone

2. How is a tropical zone different from a temperate zone? Circle all answers that apply.

   a. Tropical zones are dry all year.

   b. Tropical zones are hot all year.

   c. Tropical zones receive rain most of the year.

   d. Tropical zones are closer to the equator.

   e. Tropical zones are only in jungles.

3. An unusual warming of the tropical area of the Pacific Ocean can cause flooding in some areas and droughts in other areas. What is this event called?

   a. La Niña

   b. volcanic eruption

   c. El Niño

   d. blackberry winter

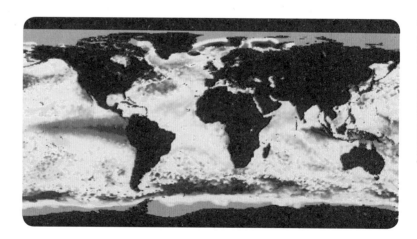

4. Look at the data in the table. What is the climate type?

Now, use the data to predict the climate in 2020 by identifying temperature and precipitation patterns.

	2010		2011		2012		2020	
	Temp (°F)	Precip (in.)	Temp (°F)	Precip (in.)	Temp (°F)	Precip (in.)	Temp (°F)	Precip (in.)
Spring	37	2	36	2	38	2		
Summer	78	1	82	1	79	1		
Fall	38	1	37	2	39	2		
Winter	19	1	18	1	20	1		

5. Which of the following describe climate? Circle all answers that apply.

   a. weather experienced day to day

   b. average yearly rainfall

   c. daily rainfall

   d. average yearly temperature

   e. daily temperature

   f. monthly weather

6. Circle all of the items that can cause temporary differences in the climate in some areas.

   a. Mountains elevate an area higher than the area around it.

   b. Melting ice releases cool air in a region.

   c. Volcanic eruptions blow out a lot of ash into the air.

   d. La Niña lowers temperatures in the Pacific Ocean.

   e. El Niño raises temperatures in the Pacific Ocean along Central and South America.

   f. Shade caused by clouds cools off the area.

Unit Review

Use the map to answer
questions 1 and 2.

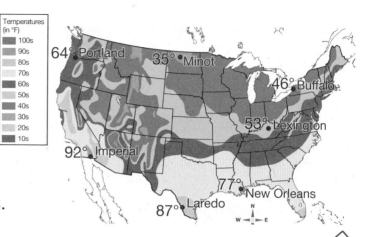

1. Select three cities. Make
a bar graph that shows the
temperatures of those cities.

2. What season is shown? Use information from the map
as evidence to support your argument.

_____

_____

3. Circle all the types of dangerous weather associated
with winter.

   a. hurricanes   **c.** tornadoes

   b. blizzards   **d.** ice storms

4. Circle the choice that does not name a climate zone.

   a. polar   **c.** dry

   b. tropical   **d.** temperate

5. You are completing a weather data chart for Big Bear City, CA. Write the correct letter for the temperature and precipitation in the chart.

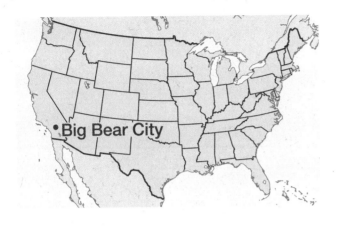

a. 3 in. of rain   **b.** 35 in. of snow   **c.** 34 °F   **d.** 63 °F

	Summer	Winter
Average temperature was:		
Total precipitation was:		

6. Circle the statement that describes a climate rather than weather.

    a. The sky has been cloudy all week.

    b. It will be dry today and then rain tomorrow.

    c. The wind died down once the storm passed.

    d. It is hot in the summer and mild in the winter.

7. Explain how meteorologists are able to make predictions about the weather. Use evidence to defend your claim on the lines below.

8. During a hurricane, windows may shatter due to strong winds and flying debris. This is dangerous to the people inside. Identify one constraint and two criteria for solutions that address this problem.

9. Evaluate three possible solutions to the problem in Question 8. Identify the pros and cons of each solution.

	Nail plastic over your windows.	Use shatter-proof glass in windows.	Add retractable metal window shutters.
Pros			
Cons			

10. Use evidence to support an argument for the best solution.

Interactive Glossary

As you learn about each item, add notes, drawings, or sentences in the extra space. This will help you remember what the terms mean. Here's an example:

fungi (FUHN•jee) A group of organisms that get nutrients by decomposing other organisms.

Mushrooms are a type of fungi.

Glossary Pronunciation Key

With every Glossary term, there is also a phonetic respelling. A phonetic respelling writes the word the way it sounds, which can help you pronounce new or unfamiliar words. Use this key to help you understand the respellings.

Sound	As in	Phonetic Respelling
a	bat	(BAT)
ah	lock	(LAHK)
air	rare	(RAIR)
ar	argue	(AR•gyoo)
aw	law	(LAW)
ay	face	(FAYS)
ch	chapel	(CHAP•uhl)
e	test	(TEST)
	metric	(MEH•trik)
ee	eat	(EET)
	feet	(FEET)
	ski	(SKEE)
er	paper	(PAY•per)
	fern	(FERN)
eye	idea	(eye•DEE•uh)
i	bit	(BIT)
ing	going	(GOH•ing)
k	card	(KARD)
	kite	(KYT)
ngk	bank	(BANGK)

Sound	As in	Phonetic Respelling
oh	over	(OH•ver)
oo	pool	(POOL)
ow	out	(OWT)
oy	foil	(FOYL)
s	cell	(SEL)
	sit	(SIT)
sh	sheep	(SHEEP)
th	that	(THAT)
	thin	(THIN)
u	pull	(PUL)
uh	medal	(MED•uhl)
	talent	(TAL•uhnt)
	pencil	(PEN•suhl)
	onion	(UHN•yuhn)
	playful	(PLAY•fuhl)
	dull	(DUHL)
y	yes	(YES)
	ripe	(RYP)
z	bags	(BAGZ)
zh	treasure	(TREZH•er)

adaptation
(ad•uhp•TAY•shuhn) A trait or characteristic that helps an organism survive. **(p. 161)**

adaptación Rasgo o característica que ayuda a un organismo a sobrevivir.

aquatic (uk•KWO•tik) Something that exists in or on water. **(p. 208)**

acuático Que existe en o sobre el agua.

balanced forces
(BAL•uhnst FAWRS•iz) Forces that cancel each other out because they are equal in size and opposite in direction. **(p. 36)**

fuerzas equilibradas Condición que ocurre cuando todas las fuerzas se cancelan por ser fuerzas iguales y opuestas.

camouflage (KAM•uh•flazh) An adaptation that allows an organism to blend in with its surroundings. **(p. 166)**

camuflaje Adaptación que le permite a un organismo mimetizarse con su entorno.

climate (KLY•muht) The pattern of weather an area experiences over a long period of time. **(p. 268)**

clima Patrón de tiempo que experimenta una región durante largos periodos.

constraint (KUHN•straint) A real-world limit on the resources of a solution such as available time, money, or materials. **(p. 5)**

restricción Algo que limita u obstaculiza.

criteria (kry•TEER•ee•uh) The desired features of a solution. **(p. 5)**

criterios Estándares para medir el éxito.

electricity
(ee•lek•TRIH•sih•tee)
A form of energy. People
produce electricity by
using energy from other
sources. **(p. 74)**

electricidad Una forma
de energía.

engineer (en•juh•NEER)
A person who uses science and math to
design structures, machines, and systems to
solve problems. **(p. 11)**

ingeniero Persona que utiliza las
matemáticas y las ciencias para diseñar
tecnología que resuelva algún problema.

environment
(en•VY•ruhn•muhnt) All
the living and nonliving
things that surround
and affect an organism.
(p. 142)

medio ambiente Todos
los seres vivos y no vivos
que rodean y afectan a un
organismo.

extinct (ek•STINGKT) Describes organisms that are no longer found living on Earth. **(p. 205)**

extinto Describe organismos que ya no habitan en la Tierra.

force (FAWHRS) A push or a pull, which may cause a change in an object's motion. **(p. 30)**

fuerza Empujón o tirón que puede causar un cambio en el movimiento de un objeto.

fossil (FAHS•uhl) The remains or traces of an organism that lived long ago. **(p. 194)**

fósil Restos o rastros que deja un organismo que vivió hace mucho tiempo.

friction (FRIK•shuhn) A force that slows or stops things that are touching. **(p. 34)**

fricción Una fuerza que hace que objetos en contacto se muevan más despacio o se dejen de mover.

habitat (HAB•ih•tat) A place where an organism lives and can find everything it needs to survive. **(p. 163)**

hábitat Lugar donde vive un organismo y donde puede encontrar todo lo que necesita para sobrevivir.

hazard (HAZ•urd) Something that can cause damage to a person or property. **(p. 250)**

riesgo Algo que puede causar daño a una persona o un bien.

© Houghton Mifflin Harcourt Publishing Company • Image Credits:

life cycle (LYF SY•kuhl) Changes that happen to an animal or a plant during its life. **(p. 89)**

ciclo de vida Etapas que experimenta un ser vivo en la medida que crece y se transforma.

M

magnet (MAG•nit) An object that attracts iron and a few other—but not all—metals. **(p. 62)**

imán Objeto que atrae el hierro y algunos otros metales (pero no todos).

mimicry (MIHM•ih•kree) An adaptation that allows an animal to protect itself by looking like another kind of animal or like a plant. **(p. 166)**

mimetismo Adaptación que le permite a un animal protegerse, al tomar el aspecto de otro tipo de animal o planta.

net force (NET FAWHRS)
The combination of all of the forces acting on an object. **(p. 37)**

fuerza neta La combinación de todas las fuerzas que actúan sobre un objeto.

offspring (AWF•spring)
The young of a plant or animal. **(p. 110)**

Cría (retoño) – Animal joven (o planta joven).

Retoño (cría) – Planta joven (o animal joven).

organism
(AWR•guh•niz•uhm)
A living thing. **(p. 86)**

organismo Ser vivo.

patterns of motion
(PAT•urnz UHF MO•shuhn)
When the same motion
repeats over and over.
(p. 53)

**patrones de
movimiento** Cuando el
mismo movimiento se
repite una y otra vez.

population
(pahp•yuh•LAY•shuhn)
All of the members of a
certain kind of plant or
animal in an environment.
(p. 92, 174)

población Todos los
miembros de un cierto
tipo de planta o animal en
un ambiente.

technology
(tek•NAHL•uh•jee)
Engineered products and
processes that meet a
want or need. **(p. 11)**

tecnología Diseño de
productos y procesos
que cumplen con una
necesidad o un requisito.

terrestrial
(TUH•rest•ree•uhl) Something that exists in or on land. **(p. 209)**

terrestre Que existe en o sobre la tierra.

traits (TRAYTZ) Physical characteristics of a person, animal, or plant. **(p. 110)**

rasgo Características físicas de una persona, animal o planta.

unbalanced forces
(uhn•BAL•uhnst FAWRS•iz) Forces that cause a change in an object's motion because they don't cancel each other out. **(p. 36)**

fuerzas desequilibradas Fuerzas que provocan un cambio en el movimiento de un objeto porque ellas no se cancelan entre sí.

Index

Index

F

G

H

Index

Index

availability of resources, 174
behaviors, 159, 163, 164
by blending in, 145
camouflage for, 122
in environment, 121, 124, 129, 165
in groups, 125, 131
structures that help, 156

T

teamwork, 16
technology, 11, 12
  improving, 10, 11
temperate zone, 270
temperature, 232, 271, 272
  change, 224, 227, 231
terrestrial ecosystem, 209, 210
testing a solution, 7, 17, 18, 19, 21
thunderstorm, 228, 247
tornado, 246, 247, 249
Tornado Alley, 247
toy train, 54
traits, 110, 111, 112, 115, 116, 117
  affect finding a mate, 128
  affect reproduction, 128
  animal, 149, 150
  helpful or harmful, 128
  organism, 142
  pattern, 115
  plants, 149
  for safety, 133
  survival, 128, 129, 161
tree
  adult, 94
  apple, 94
  mangrove, 167
  petrified, 202
  pine, 96, 97, 182
  sand live oak, 167
  young, 94
tropical zone, 270
tug of war, 36, 37

U

unbalanced forces, 36
Unit Review, 24–26, 80–82, 136–138, 216–218, 278–280
Upernavik Greenland, 272
upward force, 42

V

Van de Graff machine, 76, 77
vertical-slot fish passage, 187
volcano, 181, 274

W

wants and needs, 11
watering plants, 3, 4, 15, 17
watering spike, 15
weather, 220, 221, 249, 268
  change, 224, 228
  in Chicago, 228
  condition, 228, 231
  dangers, 242
  data, 225
  differences, 262
  on Earth, 260
  modeled, 255
  patterns, 222, 234, 259
  patterns, differences, 261, 265
  predict, 221, 227, 231, 232, 250
  radar and satellites, 250
  regional, 225
  severe, 242, 246, 247, 251
  sunny, 222
weight, 42
wildfire, 180, 182
wind
  effect of, 240
  pattern, 240
wind direction, 229
wind machine, 238, 249, 254, 255
  purpose, 241

winter, 228
work together, 20. *See also* teamwork

Y

young tree, 94

Z

zero net, force, 37
zipline, 39

COLOR Me! Engineering robot

I am a scientist.

COLOR Me!

Science is FUN!

COLOR Me! Earth Science robot

You're on a ROLL!

COLOR Me! Life Science robot

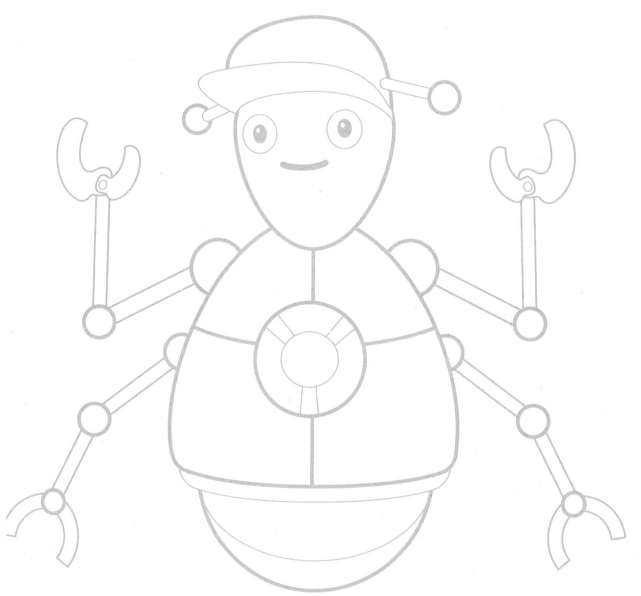

Science is COOL!